Welcome To The ZONE
Peak Performance Redefined

Scott Ford

outskirtspress
DENVER, COLORADO

The opinions expressed in this manuscript are solely the opinions of the author and do not represent the opinions or thoughts of the publisher. The author has represented and warranted full ownership and/or legal right to publish all the materials in this book.

Welcome To The Zone
Peak Performance Redefined
All Rights Reserved.
Copyright © 2014 Scott Ford
v4.0

Cover Photo © 2014 Sara Ford. All rights reserved - used with permission.

This book may not be reproduced, transmitted, or stored in whole or in part by any means, including graphic, electronic, or mechanical without the express written consent of the publisher except in the case of brief quotations embodied in critical articles and reviews.

Outskirts Press, Inc.
http://www.outskirtspress.com

ISBN: 978-1-4787-0652-6

Outskirts Press and the "OP" logo are trademarks belonging to Outskirts Press, Inc.

PRINTED IN THE UNITED STATES OF AMERICA

Table of Contents

Introduction: Playing Tennis In The Zone i

    I.1: A Brief Look at the Zone   i
    I.2: Is this Book for You?   iv
    I.3: What To Expect   v
    I.4: The Steps   viii
    I.5: Support   x

PHASE I: Core Concept: Getting In The Zone 1

Chapter 1: Serial Mode and Parallel Mode 3

    1.1: The Inner Game   3
    1.2: The Characteristics of Normal and Peak Performance   5
    1.3: Switching Modes of Operation   8
    1.4: Goals   9
    1.5: Positive and Negative Contact   10
    1.6: Traditional Teaching Approaches   12
    1.7: Right Time – Right Place   13

Chapter 2: A Different Set of Fundamentals 30

    2.1: The Contact Sequence   30
    2.2: The Contact Zone   32
    2.3: The Three Faces of Timing   35
    2.4: The Primary Contact Point   37
    2.5: The Contact Quadrants   39
    2.6: How To Objectively Measure Your Timing   40

Chapter 3: Fixing Your Focus 46

    3.1: Fixed Focus and the Zone   46
    3.2: Serial Mode and Parallel Mode   47

3.3: Focused Eyes – Focused Mind	50
3.4: A Visual Analogy	54
3.5: Two Opposing Visual Strategies	57

Chapter 4: Serving in the Zone 71

4.1: The Dimensions of the Serving Zone	71
4.2: The Serving Sequence	72
4.3: The 3-Point on the Serve.	74
4.4: Calling Your Contact Point on the Serve	74
4.5: Focusing Your Eyes On the 3-Point	75
4.6: Alignment at Contact	77
4.7: Three Basic Serves	77

PHASE II: Core Concept: Maintaining the Zone 81

Chapter 5: Playing in the Present. 83

5.1: Connecting to the Present Dimension	83
5.2: Temporal Location	86
5.3: The Zone and Time	88
5.4: Serial and Parallel Interface	89
5.5: Letting Go of the Past	90
5.6: Flash-Outs	92
5.7: Future Focus and Anticipation	94
5.8: Two Visual Pathways of the Brain	96
5.9: Heightened Visual Awareness	99

Chapter 6: Change. 110

6.1: The Zone and Sport Psychology	110
6.2: Being in the Present	113
6.3: Hitting the 3-Point	115
6.4: Operation	121

PHASE III: Core Concept: Competing in the Zone 129

Chapter 7: Competition 131
    7.1: Coming Out of a Parallel Mode   131
    7.2: Leaving the Past Where It Belongs   135
    7.3: Trust – Fear - Ego   138
    7.4: Competition vs. Rivalry   141
    7.5: Outcome-Based Competition   143
    7.6: Process vs. Outcome   143
    7.7: Winning the Real Competition   145
    7.8: Seek and Ye Shall Find   147
    7.9: The Spiritual Dimension of Tennis   149
    7.10: The Now Drill   151

Chapter 8: Competing in the Zone 162
    8.1: The Battle   162
    8.2: Controlling Your Emotions   164
    8.3: The Parallel Mode Process   166
    8.4: The Full Potential Experience   169

Bibliography 173

Acknowledgements

I would like to acknowledge the help of several experts for their assistance over the years in the development of the Parallel Mode Process. William Hines, M.D. (Ophthalmology) for his initial help in understanding the visual differences between Variable-Depth of Focus and Fixed-Depth of Focus visual input patterns; Michael Mesches, Ph.D.(behavioral neuroscience) for his immeasurable assistance in helping me to understand and better define the connection between playing in the zone and the visual pathways of the brain; Othon Kesend, Ph.D. (sports psychology) for his help in defining the psychological aspects of the Parallel Mode Process; Darlene Kluka, Ph.D. (motor learning) for her sports vision expertise.

I would also like to thank Kurt Desautels of the USTA, Colorado Division for his co-authorship of the Parallel Mode Manual, a short-course in playing tennis in the zone; Randy Ross, USPTA and Gay West, USPTA for their assistance and open-minded professionalism; Lew Kosich, USPTA, MS, CPT and former President of the Colorado Division of the USPTA for his invaluable critiques and technical assistance; and a big thanks to Dr. Jim Loehr, whose support over the last 30 years has helped me on my own journey into the zone. Thanks to Antonio Cicarelli for his original web graphics, Tyler Ford for his art direction, Sara Ford for her cover photography, and Cindy Sewick for redesigning the graphics for print.

A special thanks to Dorothy Stein, Ed.D. for her editorial assistance with this book.

Finally, I would like to thank my wife, Jane for being the best part of my life.

Foreword

By David W. Smith

The concept of helping players reach their potential is a lofty goal for any instructor. Because true player-potential is defined by so many intrinsic and extrinsic factors, a tennis player must look beyond the idiosyncrasies of stroke technique and methodology to achieve personal success and move closer to their true playing potential. Likewise, instructors must be in tune with the best patterns that move players forward in progressive improvement.

This is where Scott Ford's book, "Welcome to the Zone," fills the often common void that ties technical aspects of tennis with the patterns associated with the mental processes that players need to master for ultimate success.

The Parallel Mode Process that Scott Ford has developed and tested is truly a practical means to maximize performance in both achieving higher levels of stroke production as well as competing at optimal levels. In my 35 years of teaching tennis I've never had a process that is not only effective for ALL levels of players, but one that is an easily achievable method to understand and apply by all students. The steps which Scott outlines in this book will indeed have a profound effect on players as they train, as they practice, and as they compete.

I encourage every player—and coach—to study the tenants that Scott has detailed and prescribed within these pages. Through his insatiable thirst for developing championship competitors, Scott has diligently pursued higher consciousness as well as on-court evaluation to the point that such advice is pure performance magic!

I have used his Parallel Mode Process in nearly every lesson over the past eight years since I first learned these patterns and tools from Scott. I've seen the advantages such insights have provided my students on the learning court. But, perhaps more enlightening, I've witnessed the response of students who employ these same methods in competitive play. Such responses have been resounding…if not literally enlightening for so many.

Give this information the attention it deserves. You certainly won't regret the time spent. And you WILL certainly see the results in your game.

David W. Smith
Senior Editor, TennisOne.com
Author, TENNIS MASTERY & COACHING MASTERY
Dunlop Master Professional
USPTA

Preface: A Different Tennis Journey

"The accidental reveals man."
— Pablo Picasso

My journey into the zone began quite by accident. In 1978, while hitting with a psychologist friend of mine, I did something on the tennis court that caused me to go into the zone. The zone is a colloquial term for the human peak performance experience, also referred to as a "flow state." I was completely surprised when it happened because I had never before been able to play tennis in the zone on purpose. When I did get into the zone, which was occasionally, it always seemed to happen by chance, not choice. As if the zone had a mind of its own and I had no say in the matter.

But on that particular day, for some reason, this childlike, imaginary thing I was doing was causing me to go into the zone every time I did it. My friend immediately noticed the difference.

"What just happened to you?" he asked.

So I showed him what I was doing and he tried it. To my surprise, he, too, started playing tennis in the zone! The level of his performance instantly skyrocketed and we both started playing at our highest level. When we finished I asked him what he thought had happened. He said he wasn't sure, but he had some books on human consciousness that might help explain this magical phenomenon.

That same day I started to study the zone, and along with being able to study the zone from the outside by reading about it, I found that I could also study the zone from the inside by doing it. It made sense to me that the best way to understand an experience was through experiencing it firsthand, so I kept putting myself in the zone using this accidental technique I had chanced upon, and by experiencing this peak performance state day after day, I was able to make observations I could not make from outside the experience.

As I shared these observations with other players, I noticed them looking at me like I was off my rocker. But when they tried it, they also went into the zone. It was like watching people going through a series of "Aha!" experiences right in front of my eyes. Obviously, the most noticeable difference was the heightened level of performance they experienced when they went into the zone, but there was something else happening that was deeper than the improvement in performance. Something was happening to them, and me, at a core level. I couldn't explain it, but I knew that this experience was the essence of the game. As Billie Jean King once said about playing tennis in the zone, "this is what the game is all about."

Little did I know at the time that being in the zone is not only what the game of tennis is all about, but that being in the zone is also what the game of life is all about.

As strange as that sounded to me at first, when I looked at the bigger picture, I found that the game of tennis and the game of life had more than a few metaphorical similarities. I started looking at the competitions I faced every day of my life. I looked at the challenges, the problem-solving and decision-making situations I encountered daily. I started seeing tennis as a revved-up version of life. All the physical components were there, just like life. The emotional and mental components were there as well. And, as I was finding out, when I was in the zone, I sensed a spiritual component that was absent in my normal performance state.

Introduction: Playing Tennis In The Zone

Key Subjects:
I.1: A Brief Look at the Zone
I.2: Is this Book for You?
I.3: What To Expect
I.4: Steps
I.5: Support

I.1: A Brief Look at the Zone

The zone goes by different names. It's known as a peak performance experience. It's also called a flow experience. In Zen its called satori, an awakening. In Greece, the athletes of the Ancient Olympiad called it arete, meaning excellence in all things. But whatever you want to call it, if you have experienced the zone in any sport, you will remember it. You will remember:

- The effortless ease with which you played the game.
- How everything came together.
- How every aspect of your game started working.
- How you didn't think, you just performed.
- It was like going on automatic pilot.

At long last, you were playing the game the way you knew you could play the game:

- Your concentration was total, your focus absolute.
- You saw the ball more clearly than ever before.
- Sometimes it appeared to move in slow motion.
- You felt a sense of power and control, like you were in charge, not your opponent. In fact, you hardly noticed your opponent at all.
- You lost track of time. What seemed like minutes turned out to be an hour.
- Your reflexes were quicker, your reactions faster.

Best of all, you thoroughly enjoyed what you were doing. Winning and losing played no part in your thinking. You had a great time just playing the game. One you would remember long after the match ended.

Welcome to playing tennis "in the zone."

The next time you went out to play, however, no matter how hard you tried to reproduce the zone, you couldn't do it. Your game returned to normal:

- Your strokes were the same as always.
- The flow was gone.
- The automatic pilot was gone.
- Your concentration wavered.
- Your focus was confused.
- The ball seemed to be moving faster.
- Your opponent seemed more talented.

Where is all the control and power you felt before? What happened to those quick reflexes, that speedy reaction time? Why is the match taking so long? Where's the enjoyment? Where's the fun? Where's the zone?

Welcome back to playing tennis "in the norm."

Why is it that you were in the zone one day and in the norm the next? What were you doing differently when you were in the zone? You're the same person, with the same physical, emotional, mental, and spiritual make up. So, why is it that one day you were in the zone and the next day you weren't? What makes playing in the zone so elusive? Why is the zone such a mystery?

Modern sport psychology suggests that the door to the zone is opened when certain higher-order behavioral and environmental components are brought together simultaneously. These are called "flow components." However, there is no guarantee that synthesizing these flow components will cause the zone to happen. It will only set the stage for the possible occurrence of the zone - maybe.

In short, the general consensus is that the zone cannot be manufactured through some generic formula for peak performance. The zone can't be switched on and off at will.

My playing and teaching experiences over the past four decades suggest a completely different perspective. A perspective in which you absolutely can switch the zone on and off at will, and that there is, indeed, a generic formula for this higher-order peak performance state.

This book outlines that formula. It is a step-by-step process for learning:

- How to get into the zone.
- How to maintain the zone.
- How to compete in the zone.

This learning process doesn't happen overnight. It takes time and practice, just like anything else. If you are only interested in the outcome and winning is all that matters, then this book is probably not for you. Although you will find that you win more often when you are playing tennis in the zone than when you are playing tennis in the norm.

But this book is not about winning and losing. It's about the human operating system performing on the tennis court in its highest-order performance state. When you perform in your peak performance state, winning and losing are secondary. What matters most is that you have taken part in something very special between you and the game of tennis.

Along the way, not only will you experience a different view of what the game is all about, you will also get the rare opportunity to experience a different view of what you are all about as a human being.

I.2: Is this Book for You?

Do you ever feel:

- Lost out there on the court?
- Like nothing you are doing is working?
- Like your opponent is in control, not you?
- Like the ball isn't going where you want it to go?
- Or that you just can't put all the pieces of your game together?

If so, then this book is for you.
Do you ever feel:

- Like your game is in a rut?
- Like you are spinning your tennis wheels, practicing but not improving as rapidly as you think you should improve?
- Like your game is played between narrow margins separating the good days from the bad days and you seldom, if ever, experience the great days?
- Do you change teaching pros frequently in the hopes that a

- new pro will be the answer to your problems?
- How about a change in racquets or shoes or grips?
- Maybe your strings are too loose. Maybe they're too tight.

If these changes aren't helping your game, then this book is for you.

Playing tennis in the zone is not about the stroking techniques you learned from your last teaching pro. Playing in the zone is not about the strategies you learned from watching professional tennis. The zone has nothing to do with racquets or shoes or string tension. The zone is about the human operating system, not the tools with which it operates. If you are interested in your own operating system and how it can work more efficiently and more accurately on the tennis court, then this book is for you.

We tend to change everything we can possibly change in an effort to achieve a higher level of performance. But what we don't change is the one thing that is truly causal to performance improvement, and that is to change the basic way we use our eye/brain/body operating system on the tennis court; to change the way we use the underlying Input, Processing, Output (IPO) dynamics of our sensorimotor operating system.

In other words, by improving the way your operating system interfaces with the tennis environment, you will improve your performance on the court. This book will show you how to improve the interface between your operating system and the tennis environment in which you operate.

I.3: What To Expect

Learning to play tennis in the zone is an adventure that is empowering as well as frustrating, enjoyable as well as maddening. The main challenge in learning how to play tennis in the zone has nothing to do with tennis. Rather, it deals with the process of change at the most fundamental of human levels: the human operating system and the core changes to your physical, emotional, mental, and spiritual behaviors brought about by a higher-order interface with the tennis environment. At first, you can expect to experience confusion, disbelief, loss, grief, and anger. Sounds like fun; doesn't it? Not exactly what you had in mind for a peak experience, right? But that's the downside of learning anything involving change:

- It can be discouraging.
- The downside tells you to quit.
- The old way is easier.
- The old way works just fine.
- I can't make these changes.
- It's too hard, too demanding, too different.

So you can expect to experience a downside. But there is also an upside. And if you don't give up on your ability to control your own operating system, you will get to experience the upside of playing tennis in the zone.

- You will experience what it's like to play in your most efficient and accurate operating mode.
- You will experience what it's like to form a one-to-one relationship with the game of tennis. And that one-to-one relationship with the game is an experience you will soon come to treasure.

There is, however, a fundamental sacrifice you must make in order to play tennis in the zone. Simply put, you have to give up playing tennis in the norm. This doesn't mean you will forget how to play tennis. It just means that in order to engage your operating system in its peak performance state, you must first disengage it from its normal performance state. You must detach from playing tennis in the norm, and detaching from your normal performance state means you must also detach from your normal behavioral state. That detachment will not come easily at first.

Expect to be separated from your comfort zone. Playing in the zone does not mean playing in your "comfort zone." On the contrary, you should expect the unexpected. You must be willing to venture into the unknown, and that means one thing will surely happen: you will experience fear – the fear of the unknown. Expect it.

In large part, this book is about confronting your own fears. Fear of failure, fear of success, fear of change. These fears are present in all of us, and if you want to switch from playing tennis in the norm to playing tennis in the zone, you will have to confront your fears. So, expect confrontation.

Expect failure. Failure is part of growth and development. You had failures when you were learning to play tennis in the norm, right? Why would you expect anything different when you are learning to play tennis in the zone? No one learns how to play tennis in the zone without experiencing failures. Yet, even knowing this, I've had players come out for one lesson, get into the zone and say, "Okay, I've got it now," then lose it shortly thereafter, give up, and return to the narrow margins of their normal performance state. Had they given up that soon after a failure at playing in the norm, they might have given up the game of tennis altogether.

There is no reason to give up after a failure at playing in the zone. It's like giving up on your peak performance state just because you weren't perfect the first time. You must expect failure. Allow failure. Failure is necessary for success. It must not be feared, but rather welcomed as integral to the process of change.

Expect, also, success - unimaginable success. The success you experienced on those rare occasions when you found yourself inexplicably in the zone. As you go through the steps in this book, you will start to understand what causes you to enter the zone, and you will begin to reproduce and maintain your peak performance state for longer periods of time. Expect it; expect success. It, too, is an integral part of the process of change, and much easier to welcome than failure.

There are other changes waiting for you when you start playing tennis in the zone, but for the most part you can expect the experience to feel distinctly different. Playing tennis in the zone is not the same as playing tennis in the norm. Your peak performance state is not the same as your normal performance state, and when you change to your peak performance state, you get a simultaneous change in your overall behavioral state.

So you can expect:

- A different physical experience;
- A different emotional experience;
- A different mental experience;
- A different spiritual experience.

I.4: The Steps

Learning to play tennis in the zone can only be done experientially. Reading about the zone is not the same as being in the zone. With your peak performance state, you learn by doing. You have to practice being in the zone, and that practice starts with easy exercises that progress into more challenging experiences with your peak performance state.

Throughout this book there are specific on-court exercises, *steps* designed to put you in the zone, which means they are guaranteed to take you out of your comfort zone. They will seem illogical at first. That's what should happen. Remember, playing tennis in the zone will not feel the same as playing tennis in the norm. If you feel normal doing these exercises, then you're not doing them properly. If, however, you feel a little strange during the process, then relax, you're right on track. By definition, playing tennis in the zone is out of the ordinary. Also out of the ordinary are the steps you will go through to make the switch from your normal performance state to your peak performance state.

The steps in each chapter will take you deeper into the zone, each step building on the previous one. You should experience each of these steps fully before moving to the next. Their sequence will allow you to experience deeper changes in your physical, emotional, mental and spiritual behaviors.

Detaching from your normal behavioral state and connecting with your peak behavioral state is necessary for playing any sport in the zone. Tennis just happens to be one of the templates upon which you can experience these peak or flow behaviors. If you do these steps in order, each one will reveal more of the core behavioral changes that are occurring in your game. These changes will occur over time, some faster than others. You will soon come to recognize the higher-order flow behaviors that accompany your peak performance state. As you become more aware of these changes, you will also begin to recognize that there is much more to the game of tennis than you ever before imagined.

In moving through the steps, there will not only be physical changes occurring in the efficiency and accuracy of your game, but you will also experience a growing ability to control your emotions and get off the roller-coaster ride of emotional instability. Mentally, you will find yourself changing from a player who is constantly fighting with distractions and concentrative lapses, to a player who knows exactly how to focus and, more importantly, on what to focus exactly. Finally, you will awaken the most mysterious and misunderstood dimension of your game; you will awaken the dimension of your game left dormant and undeveloped. The dimension of your game you never talk about - the spiritual dimension. You know it's there; you're just not sure how to get to it. These steps will show you how to experience the spiritual dimension of tennis.

Other components of the zone experience will also become more obvious as you go through the steps in this book. They will be discussed in each chapter, and it is suggested that you discuss them further with your practice partner or practice group. To be fully understood, these changes need to be talked about and shared. Different perspectives will arise in your discussions, and you will often find answers to your questions in the views of others.

I.5: Support

Whenever we undertake major changes in our lives, we often seek out the support of friends or counselors. Support systems are everywhere in western society, ranging from colleagues to parents, friends to partners. The local phone book contains support groups of every conceivable flavor. Support systems are invaluable in the process of change, any change, and it's no different when you are changing from playing tennis in the norm to playing tennis in the zone. Like anything else, it's hard to change in the vacuum of isolation, so I always suggest to my students that they find a willing practice partner with whom they can practice the steps in each chapter.

Better yet, if your practice partner also wants to learn how to play tennis in the zone, then you've got a built-in support system. It always helps if you practice with someone who understands the changes you are going through. How better than to find someone willing to make the changes with you?

PHASE I
Core Concept: Getting In The Zone

First Things First. Before you can play tennis in the zone, you have to first get in the zone. Exactly what does that mean? What, exactly, is the zone and why is it more desirable to play tennis in the zone than "in the norm?"

Phase I is all about getting in the zone using a process I've developed called "The Parallel Mode Process" or PMP for short.

Chapter 1: Serial Mode and Parallel Mode

"Imagination is more important than knowledge."
— Albert Einstein

Key Subjects
1.1: The Inner Game
1.2: The Characteristics of Normal and Peak Performance
1.3: Switching Modes of Operation
1.4: Goals
1.5: Positive and Negative Contact.
1.6: Traditional Teaching Approaches
1.7: Right Time – Right Place

1.1: The Inner Game

Whenever I teach people how to play tennis in the zone, I feel like I am standing on the shoulders of giants in this field of peak performance and the zone. One of the first people to discuss this subject in any depth was Timothy Gallwey. His *Inner Game of Tennis* was groundbreaking in its approach to human performance through the perspective of Zen philosophy and the synthesis of mind and body through relaxed concentration.

At the time Gallwey came out with *The Inner Game*, I was becoming an expert in the outer game. To me the whole notion of teaching an inner game was hogwash. I was a perfect example of the teaching pro who fed his students a full plate of biomechanically sound techniques, all the while feeling remarkably good about my teaching, even though my students didn't improve as fast as I thought they should given the expert instruction they were receiving.

As an instructor, I could break down a player's strokes with the best of them, detecting the smallest technical errors, then demonstrating a variety of corrections from which they could choose. The more errors I could detect, the more my teacher's ego grew and the more bang my students thought they were getting for their buck. They came to lessons expecting to fix the errors in the parts of their game, and, by so doing, fix their whole game.

The logic was solid, based on linear system dynamics. The traditional approach to teaching tennis that says: *the dynamics of the parts of a system determine the behavior of the whole system.*

In tennis, this means that if the dynamics of the parts of your game are correct then the behavior of your whole game will also be correct.

I loved this concept! It was like money in the bank. I could always find errors in someone's game, and by detecting and correcting errors in the parts of their game, they naturally assumed they were correcting the behavior of their whole game; a logical assumption according to the traditional teaching paradigm. It made terrific sense both pedagogically and monetarily. I could easily spend the rest of my life making a handy living detecting and correcting errors in the various parts of a player's game.

There was only one problem. This methodology didn't work very well. Yes, players got better with practice, but something was missing. Their performance was never as good as I thought it should be, nor was it as good as they thought it should be. When I watched them play, I saw them making many of the same errors they were making before they took a lesson in how to correct those errors.

What was going wrong? Weren't they listening? Was there something wrong with them as learners? Or could there be something wrong with my teaching?

I certainly didn't think so. My lessons were by the book. The United States Professional Tennis Association had recently certified me as a Professional-1, which meant that I was highly qualified, thoroughly tested, biomechanically sound and extremely well dressed. So why wasn't it working? Could this Gallwey guy with all his Zenny, left-coast ideology really have something?

At the time, I didn't think so. I bought into the traditional dogma that playing tennis in the zone was something that came over players only by chance. It could not be taught through some inner-transformation, nor could it be learned through Zen or any other spiritual practice. Granted, it was an intriguing idea, but as a USPTA Pro/Missouri Synod Lutheran, Zen and the art of tennis teaching was more than I could handle.

It took a personal experience with playing tennis in the zone to shake the foundations of my approach to the game of tennis as well as my approach to the game of life.

1.2: The Characteristics of Normal and Peak Performance

My own personal experience came several years after the Inner Game was published, and even though it happened through a completely different approach than Zen, the effect was the same. I achieved what is known in Zen as "satori," an awakening.

At about the same time I started investigating the zone from the inside, another of the giants in the field of peak performance was developing a new approach to this heightened state of awareness, which he called "flow."

Mihali Csikszentmihalyi, Ph.D., from the University of Chicago, interviewed hundreds of people who had experienced flow in some aspect of their lives. Through these interviews, he was able to piece together the behavioral characteristics of the flow state, and he hypothesized that by bringing together these various flow components, an athlete performing on the field or a housewife performing in the kitchen could open the door to the flow experience. He also hypothesized that while the synthesis of these flow components could make the experience of flow more of a possibility, it did not guarantee the experience would happen.

Something was still missing. Even though the zone experience was being studied scientifically, no one knew what caused it to happen. In fact, those most closely involved with the phenomenon insisted that the zone could not be created intentionally; it just happened. Humans could not control the zone; they could only prepare for it by bringing together certain behavioral and environmental characteristics.

Here is a list of flow components developed by Dr. Csikszentmihalyi. On the left are some of the normal behavioral characteristics you experience when you are playing tennis in the norm. On the right are the behavioral characteristics you will be experiencing when you switch to playing tennis in the zone.

Operationally, the difference between playing tennis in the norm and playing tennis in the zone is the difference between a "Serial Mode" of operation and a "Parallel Mode" of operation. When you are in your normal performance state, your sensorimotor operating system is interfacing with the tennis environment in a Serial Mode. But when you are in your peak performance state, your sensorimotor operating system is interfacing with the same tennis environment in a Parallel Mode.

More will be discussed about these different operating modes throughout the book, but, for now, it is sufficient to know two things:

1. That your Parallel Mode is much more efficient and more accurate as an operating mode than your Serial Mode, which accounts for the higher level of play you experience when your are in the zone.

2. That your Parallel Mode is accompanied by the higher-order behavioral state of flow, which accounts for the change you experience in your physical, emotional, mental and spiritual behaviors when you are in the zone.

SERIAL MODE CHARACTERISTICS (Playing Tennis in the Norm)	PARALLEL MODE CHARACTERISTICS (Playing Tennis in the Zone)
Confusion: Unclear goals and objectives	**Clear Goals:** Clearly set goals and objectives
Uncertainty and Doubt: Ambiguous performance feedback	**Unambiguous Feedback:** Immediate performance feedback
Lack of Concentration - Distraction: Easily distracted by events around your performance	**Total Concentration:** Detachment from all distractions; total absorption in your performance
"Paralysis by Analysis:" Over-analysis prevents instinctual behavior	**Action/Awareness Merging:** Instinctual play; the sense of going on "automatic pilot"
Loss of Confidence: Decreased sense of control, increased sense of powerlessness	**Sense of Control:** Increased sense of mastery and command over your objective
Self-Consciousness: Concern for how others view your performance; increased self-image	**Loss of Self-Consciousness:** A loss of self-concern, worries and negativity; loss of ego
Linear Time: Time as a fundamental, measurable quantity	**Transformation of Time:** Experience "time expansion" and "time contraction"
Limited Visual Awareness: Sequential visual awareness; one fixation point after another	**Increased Visual Awareness:** Heightened awareness of everything in your visual field
Normal Reaction Time: Normal amount of time between stimulus and response	**Quicker Reactions:** Less time between stimulus and response
Heterotelic Experience: Playing with ulterior motives; Playing to win or lose	**Autotelic Experience:** Intrinsic rewards; playing tennis for the sake of the game

1.3: Switching Modes of Operation

It's important to remember that your ability to play tennis in the zone has nothing to do with your ability to play tennis. I know that sounds odd, but playing tennis in the zone has to do with your ability to switch from your Serial Operating Mode to your Parallel Operating Mode. Operationally, it's that simple. Psychologically, it's a little more complicated.

In order to switch from your Serial Mode to your Parallel Mode, you must also detach from your Serial Mode behaviors and allow your Parallel Mode behaviors to take over.

Engaging your Parallel Mode behaviors does not require any talent in tennis. It requires a talent in concentration, an ability to control your visual and mental focus. You make the change from a Serial Mode to a Parallel Mode by changing the way you visually and mentally focus.

When players are confronted with this concept it sometimes catches them by surprise. Different players have different reactions to the subject of concentration and focus. Some say their concentration stinks, while others say they concentrate fairly well. It's always a mixed bag, but everyone agrees that concentration and focus play and important role in their on-court performance, yet when I ask them how often they actually practice their concentration, or how they go about improving their focus on the court, I usually get puzzled looks and vague answers.

Players will gladly spend hours on the ball machine working on their stroking technique, but when it comes to working on the technique of their concentration, they're generally clueless. It's not because players are unaware of the importance of good concentration and focus. It's just that they don't know how to practice it.

Here are some questions to ask yourself about concentration and focus:

- How do you practice your concentration and focus on the tennis court?
- On what do you focus when you practice your concentration?
- Finally, how do you know if your concentration is improving?

These questions and others are addressed in the First Step. Expect to be surprised at how easy it is to concentrate at a very high level. But don't be surprised at how hard you can make it.

1.4: Goals

Goals assist us in concentration and focus, so it is important to set very clear goals (as it states in our flow list). But what does that mean? What goals should you set?

What are your goals when you go out to play tennis? Is your goal to win? Is your goal to have fun? Is your goal to exercise and work on your tan?

Everyone who plays tennis has goals, conscious or unconscious, that relate directly to their behavior on the court. What are you trying to achieve when you take out your tennis racquet, walk onto the court and start rallying the ball back and forth across the net?

Have you ever actually thought about your goals in tennis? Not just your long-term goals, but rather your goals for the next ball coming toward you. What are you trying to achieve with that ball? Here comes the ball in your direction.

What is your goal?

1.5: Positive and Negative Contact

No matter what your goals, one thing is certain: if you plan to continue playing the game, then you must first create a *positive contact event* between the oncoming ball and your racquet. A positive contact event is a contact event that results in the ball going back over the net and into the court. If you create a *negative contact event*, the ball either goes into the net or out of bounds and the point ends abruptly.

Sorry, you lose.

Make enough negative contact and not only do you lose points; you lose games, sets and matches. Try keeping your doubles partner if you make lots of negative contact. The relationship won't last. Negative contact not only loses matches, it also loses invitations to play in future matches. In some cases - although we don't like to admit it - negative contact also loses friends.

Who wants to play with someone who always makes negative contact? It's boring, it's frustrating and it wreaks havoc on your own game. You end up playing badly just trying to make up for all of your partner's negative contact. Then you start making negative contact yourself and you blame your negative contact on your lousy partner. The last thing you want is to be paired up with the same partner the next time you play. In fact, you don't even want to be on the same court with someone who constantly makes negative contact. Negative contact completely destroys the game. After all, how can you enjoy playing when you don't get a chance to play?

Positive contact, on the other hand, does the one thing that must be done to play the game. Positive contact perpetuates the life of the rally. It keeps the ball going, keeps it in play, and when you perpetuate the rally, you have a chance to win the point, the game, the set and the match.

Positive contact is mandatory for the game of tennis. Without positive contact there is no perpetuation, and without perpetuation there is no game. There is only equipment, a few players, lots of lines and rules, but no game. The game is the result of the continuous creation of positive contact. You create positive contact, your opponent creates positive contact, and the game goes on.

If you create positive contact and your opponent creates negative contact, then the rally ends and you win the point. That's how it works. You win the point because you created positive contact one more time than your opponent.

We watch the pros and think the best way to win points is by drilling heavy topspin groundstrokes deep into the corners until we hit a clean winner. And while that's a wonderful winning strategy, the majority of tennis players on the planet make complete fools of themselves by trying to adopt that very same strategy.

Positive contact, however, even at the professional level, remains fundamentally the same. Player A creates positive contact one more time than Player B and thus wins the point. No matter how much topspin, no matter how much velocity or how much angle you put on the ball, it all boils down to the fact that you created positive contact between the ball and your racquet, and that positive contact event resulted in the ball going over the net and landing inside the lines of the court.

Make positive contact with the same quality as the pros and you'll get to play in places like Wimbledon and Roland Garros. Make positive contact with the same quality as most other players in the world and you'll get to play at the local public courts.

In essence, the quality of your contact determines the quality of the arena in which you get to compete. High quality, positive contact gets you into some very fancy arenas. Negative contact gets you into the bleachers. In the game of tennis, as in the game of life, the level of your success is measured by the quality with which you make contact.

Given the relationship of positive contact to success, it serves us well to look to the continuous creation of positive contact as the primary goal or objective of the game. Beating the crap out of your opponent, winning tournaments, collecting trophies, or just having fun – it's all based on first making positive contact. That's where the game begins.

1.6: Traditional Teaching Approaches

I used to teach all my lessons with the idea that sound biomechanical technique would result in the best contact between racquet and ball, so I based my teaching agenda on the production of biomechanically sound stroking patterns rather than on the creation of continuous positive contact.

What I found, however, was that sound stroking patterns did not necessarily equate to positive contact. My students were always fundamentally sound and their strokes always looked good, but these good looking strokes didn't always create positive contact. They would hit one or two great looking strokes over the net to some untrained hacker who kept punching the ball back to them with atrocious form.

Yet, the ball kept coming back and, sooner or later, my students would end up missing shots and losing points. And every time they missed a shot, they would go through a correction ritual of re-stroking the ball with the proper technique, as if practicing the proper technique would make that stroke work the next time they had to use it.

The hardest part for me to stomach as a teacher was that the hacker with the horrendous strokes was winning, and winning because of one fundamental reality. His lousy form was creating positive contact one more time than my biomechanically sound student.

So it was back to the linear dynamics drawing board to figure out what parts of my student's game needed to be fixed in order to fix their whole game. What could be changed so as to create more positive contact?

It's a simple question, but one that has puzzled tennis teachers since the beginning of the game. It was also a question that I was becoming less interested in answering. Even my own game was becoming less interesting. In fact, I was getting bored. Nothing I tried seemed to help, and I tried everything, even the Inner Game. But the Inner Game still didn't mix with my outer mind, so I shoved the concept of the mental approach to the side. To me, the mind game was simple:

- Concentrate on the ball.
- Focus on the ball.

I could never understand exactly what it meant to "be the ball," so I tossed that one in the trash bin as mental folly. I would stick with biomechanics or nothing. I would fix my own game with traditional USPTA teaching methodology. Break my game down, see what was wrong, then put it back together again the right way. Which is exactly what I intended to do when I accidentally happened onto something that turned my whole view of tennis upside-down.

1.7: Right Time – Right Place

Here's what happened: I was playing with a psychologist friend of mine, and as we warmed up from mid-court, dinking the ball back and forth in a game of mini-tennis, I was feeling like I normally felt, nothing out of the ordinary, but as the pace of the rally picked up, I felt like I was hitting everything late. As a result, I was mis-hitting many of my shots. My timing was terrible and I wondered if the problem with my game was my timing rather than my technique. Maybe, God forbid, I suffered from bad timing.

But how do you fix bad timing? In all the reading I had done about tennis, I had never read anything that logically explained how to correct bad timing. All I knew was that my timing was late and I needed to do something to fix it. To this day, I have no idea why I did what I did next. It was totally childlike, silly almost, yet it made immediate and complete sense to me.

For some reason I decided to imagine a big picture window spanning the court at a comfortable arm's length in front of me. It looked like this:

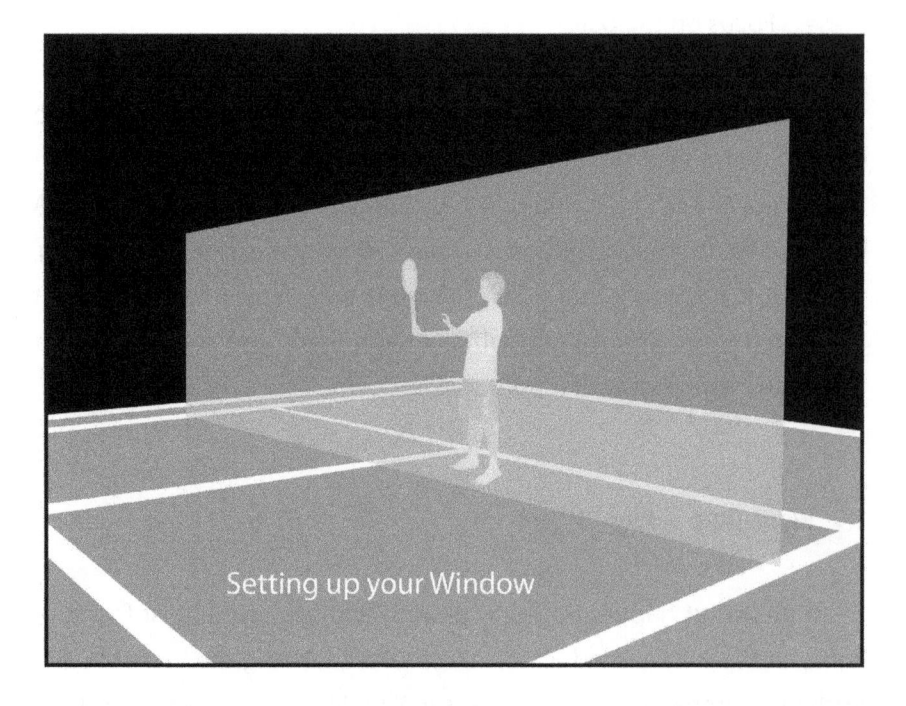

Setting up your Window

The way I figured it, if I made contact at this imaginary window, then the timing on my contact would be good, but if I made contact behind my window, then my timing would be bad. Simplistic, but it made sense:

Contact *at* my imaginary window – good timing.
Contact *behind* my imaginary window – bad timing.

So I started observing my own contact, and found that almost every ball was getting past my imaginary window before I made contact. No matter how closely I watched the ball, no matter how much I focused on it, the ball was always getting past my window. It was like I knew where the ball was, but I didn't know where my window was.

That seemed backwards to me, so I decided to do something completely different. Instead of concentrating on the ball, I started concentrating on my imaginary window. I literally visualized this great big window in front of me, and instead of using my racquet to hit the ball back over the net, I decided to use my racquet to keep all oncoming balls from getting past my imaginary window. It didn't matter to me how I did it or what my strokes looked like. As long as the ball didn't get past my window, I knew one thing for certain: the technique I used to defend my imaginary window would be perfectly timed.

I had no idea what would happen and I didn't care. My sole objective was to defend my imaginary window, and to tell myself how I was doing I simply said "yes" if I succeeded in defending my window and "no" if I didn't. I started using immediate verbal feedback to report on the success or failure of my timing.

We started another mid-court rally and I proceeded to play this child-like game of defending my imaginary window. "Yes," I would say when I was successful. "No," when the ball broke through my window.

At first, I heard myself saying, "yes – no – no – yes." My timing was erratic, but I stuck with it. It was fun and I found myself really getting into this silly game of defending my imaginary window. That's when I heard myself saying, "yes – yes – yes - yes," and to my surprise, I was volleying better than I had ever volleyed in my life.

Everything I hit was going back over the net, but I wasn't even trying to hit the ball over the net! I was simply defending my imaginary window. I was playing this simple, imaginary game and it was working better than when I played the game for real! But something else was happening at the same time, something that caused my heart to leap when I noticed it:

- I found myself totally focused on playing this imaginary game.
- I was totally absorbed in defending my window.
- My shots were effortless.
- My volleys and half-volleys were working.
- My timing was perfect.
- My movement was immediate and without thought.
- I couldn't miss.
- The ball seemed bigger; it looked like it was moving in slow motion.
- I was aware of everything that was happening on the court.

Then it hit me. I was right square in the middle of the zone.

"Whoa! Wait a minute!" I thought. This can't be true. You can't make the zone happen. Yet, here I was, right in the middle of the zone, and I knew it.

Suddenly, at the exact moment I realized what was happening, the zone left. It just went away. As quickly as it had come, it was gone, and I found myself back in my normal performance state trying to hit the ball back over the net, my timing once again late.

So I tried visualizing this window in front of me again and continued to defend it with my strokes, using yes/no feedback to ensure I was doing what I set out to do. Sure enough, it happened again. I immediately went back into the zone. I could feel it. I could sense the change in the depth of my concentration. I could feel my movement improving, my timing improving, and my contact improving.

But why? What was it about playing this imaginary game that caused me to go into the zone? What was it about changing my goal from hitting the ball over the net to defending this imaginary window that caused my performance to take an immediate and dramatic leap in efficiency and accuracy?

As I defended my imaginary window, I observed that I was making better contact than when I tried to hit the ball back over the net. This goal of defending my window was somehow causing me to make positive contact more often than when my goal was to hit the ball back over the net, and because I was making positive contact more often than usual, the ball was going back over the net more often than usual. My whole game took an immediate performance jump when I stopped trying to hit the ball over the net and started defending my imaginary window.

But how could that be? How could I hit the ball over the net without even trying? And to top it all off, I could feel myself going into this deep concentrative state we called the zone.

What was going on? Why would switching from my normal objective to this new objective cause me to go into the zone? And why, when I stopped defending my window and went back to my normal objective of trying to hit the ball over the net, did I immediately come out of the zone and return to my normal performance state?

I was even finding that I could switch back and forth at will, and all it took was a little imagination and a change of objective. To make sure I was switching from one to the other I would use the same yes/no feedback process for both.

When my objective was to hit the ball back over the net, I would focus on the ball and say "yes" when it went over the net and "no" when it didn't. (*Immediate verbal feedback on the results of my contact*).

When my objective was to defend my imaginary window, I would focus on my window and say "yes" when contact occurred at my window and "no" when contact occurred behind my window. Again, immediate verbal feedback, but this feedback was different. *It was immediate verbal feedback on the timing and location of contact, not the results of contact.*

When my objective was to hit the ball over the net, I found that I was acutely aware of the location of the ball after I hit it, but only peripherally aware of the ball at contact.

Conversely, when my objective was to defend my window, I found that I was acutely aware of every contact event but only peripherally aware of the results. I was still "seeing" my results, I just wasn't focused on them; I was focused instead on my imaginary window, and since all my contact was taking place at my imaginary window, all my contact was in focus.

Without trying to become more aware of contact, I was becoming more aware of contact, and as I became more aware of contact, the quality of my contact improved, which made for better results. The hardest part for me at first was to keep from focusing on my results and remain focused on my window. I found myself wanting to watch my own shots rather than maintaining my focus on my window. Focusing on the ball and focusing on my results was the way I normally got my success/failure feedback, but when I caught myself going back to focusing on my results, I also noticed that I came out of the zone and started playing tennis in my normal state again.

My whole concept of how to concentrate on a tennis court was getting turned upside-down, and all because this imaginary game kept putting me in the zone.

Defend my imaginary window = in the zone.
Hit the ball over the net = in the norm.

For a traditionally trained tennis teacher certified in traditional tennis teaching this was mind-boggling. I couldn't believe what was happening and yet I couldn't deny that it *was* happening. I had absolutely no reason to lie to myself about the experience. Being old-school, I never believed players could make the zone happen, so for me to immediately buy into what was happening was out of the question. We Lutherans call it the "Doubting Thomas Syndrome." I had to have proof. I had to keep doing it for myself until I could prove to myself that what was happening was really happening.

Of course, it helped to have a psychologist across the net from me who, by the way, also got in the zone when I showed him what I was doing and he tried it for himself.

"Wow! This is amazing!" he said. "You've really got something here."

I wasn't exactly sure what I had, but I was determined to study it as much as I could, and since I spent most of my days on the tennis court, I was able to study the zone on a regular basis. But teaching tennis not only gave me an opportunity to get in the zone myself and study it from the inside; it also gave me a chance to try out what I was learning about the zone with my students.

The first thing I always did, and have done with students ever since, was to have them do exactly the same thing I did when I first went into the zone, always remembering that I started at midcourt, playing mini-tennis.

I did *not* start at the baseline slugging groundstrokes back and forth with my practice partner. To this day, I always start every step with mini-tennis - midcourt to midcourt. You will see why as you go through the steps.

THE FIRST STEP
Defending Your Imaginary Window

IMPORTANT: Remember to start at mid-court. Start at the "T".

Setting up your Window

1. Visualize a big imaginary window spanning the width of the court at a comfortable arm's length in front of you. This imaginary window extends up as high as you can reach your racquet, extends down to the surface of the court, and extends to the sidelines of the court. If you move forward, your window moves forward with you; if you move back, your window moves back with you, always remaining a comfortable arm's length in front of you.

Visualizing an imaginary window in front of you requires total concentration and focus - one of the flow components.

2. Change your objective. As the ball comes toward your window, don't try to hit it back over the net. Simply use your strokes to prevent every oncoming ball from getting past your imaginary window. Defend your imaginary window with your strokes.

Defending your imaginary window with your strokes is a clear goal - another of the flow components.

3. Use immediate verbal feedback. Say "yes" if you are successful in defending your window. Say "no" if the ball gets past your window.

Saying yes or no is immediate and unambiguous feedback - another flow component.

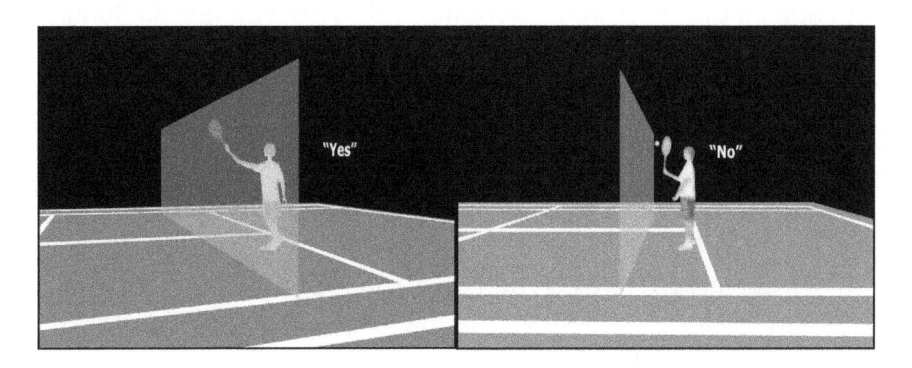

Do not judge or analyze what is going on. You will soon find out that as you continue to defend your imaginary window with your strokes, the ball starts going back over the net. It is important to let this happen without trying to make anything else happen with the ball. Remember, you are not trying to do anything with the ball other than prevent it from getting past your window with your strokes.

Also, don't get too fancy with your strokes. In the First Step, all you are doing with your strokes is using them to prevent the ball from getting past your window - nothing more, nothing less. Use your strokes to defend your window, not to hit the ball over the net. This change in objective is very important.

The last drill in the First Step involves backing up and increasing the depth of field – the distance between you and your practice partner.

As you increase the distance between players you will find yourself wanting to focus on the ball again instead of keeping your focus on your window. If you find yourself losing your focus, don't worry about it. It happens to everyone. At first, the most difficult aspect of visualizing a window at greater distances is that both the ball and your practice partner will be out of focus.

More will be discussed about the difference in visual patterns in Chapter 3, but for now, it is only important that you attempt to continuously visualize and defend your imaginary window at whatever your position on the court. In my workshops, I have the players go through the following court positions before moving on to the Second Step:

- Midcourt to Midcourt
- Backcourt to Forecourt
- Backcourt to Backcourt
- Changing depths of court

At first, you will find that it is easier to visualize your imaginary window in the midcourt and forecourt areas. Expect to lose your focus in the backcourt and when changing depths in the court. It happens to everyone. It happened to me, too. I could visualize and defend my window at midcourt and in the forecourt, but as I moved farther back into the backcourt area, I found myself losing focus on my window and going back to focusing on the ball.

When I went back to focusing on the ball, I also found myself coming out of the zone and returning to the norm. But I was determined to see if I could keep focusing on my window when I was changing depths on the court. I set my mind to keep visually and mentally focused on my imaginary window and continue to use my strokes to prevent as many balls as possible from getting past my window. With time and practice, I found that it was easier to stay visually and mentally focused on my imaginary window and let the ball come into focus as it moved toward my window and go out of focus as it moved away from my window.

Once I realized that I never lost sight of the ball, only that it moved into and out of focus, I began to relax and enjoy the process. And as I became more familiar with focusing on my window instead of the ball, I realized something else. I realized that keeping my window in focus was easier than trying to keep the ball in focus as it moved back and forth across the net. It was much easier to let the ball come into focus, contact it at my window, then let the ball go out of focus after I hit it.

Defending your imaginary window is the First Step. It takes time to learn how to keep your focus on your imaginary window while you move through the various depths of the tennis court. Don't expect to be perfect right from the start. That won't happen. But you can expect to improve with practice.

And you can expect something else, too. You can expect to experience the components of flow as you start to control your focus and change your objective. You can expect to see what it's like to get into the zone.

First Step Feedback Page

This page is all about measuring where you are in the Parallel Mode Process. By giving yourself objective feedback, you will be able to see what drills you are doing "in the zone" and which ones you are still doing "in the norm."

When I teach people how to play tennis in the zone, the First Step is specifically about learning how to *visualize and defend your imaginary window*. No emphasis is put on *outcome* in these drills, only on the *process* of using your strokes to defend this imaginary window you are visualizing at a comfortable arm's length in front of you.

The changes that take place in your operating system when you visualize and defend your imaginary window are changes that will be discussed and explained as you go through the steps of the Parallel Mode Process. For now, it is only important to know that visualizing and defending your imaginary window causes your operating system to change from a Serial Mode of Operation to a Parallel Mode of Operation, and your Parallel Mode is the underlying operating mode of your Peak Performance State.

What you are trying to measure in these early drills is your ability to give verbal "yes/no" feedback on *completing the task* of visualizing and defending your imaginary window. Notice that you are NOT giving yourself yes/no feedback on the *results* of the task you are trying to complete, only on the completion of the task itself.

If you prevent the ball from getting past your imaginary window with your strokes, say "yes". If the ball gets past your imaginary window, say "no."

Feedback Percentage

One of the terms we frequently use in the Parallel Mode Process is "feedback percentage" (FB%). FB% is defined as the ratio between the number of times you defend your imaginary window and the number of times you give yourself yes/no verbal feedback. In other words, if you defend your imaginary window ten times and you give yourself yes/no verbal feedback ten times, then your FB% was 100%.

At first, some players find immediate verbal feedback difficult and confusing, consequently their FB% is lower than they might expect. It seems like an easy thing to do, but if you are in the habit of getting your feedback by focusing on whether or not the ball goes over the net, then you are in the habit of giving yourself *outcome-based feedback*. Immediate verbal feedback on defending your imaginary window with your strokes is *process-based feedback*, and it takes time and practice before process-based feedback becomes a habit.

The higher your FB% in each of the First Step drills, the better you are getting at process-based feedback. Modern sports psychology stresses the importance of staying in the process and staying out of the outcome. The higher your FB% on the process of defending your imaginary window with your strokes, the more you are staying in the process and out of the outcome.

Self-Rating Your Progress

Once again, the three things you are measuring on the feedback page are:

1. Visualizing an imaginary window in front of you at a comfortable arm's length. (Visualize window)
2. Using your strokes to prevent the ball from getting past your

imaginary window. (Defending your window)
3. Immediate verbal "yes/no" feedback percentage (FB%)

Your rating system for visualizing and defending your imaginary window in each of the drills is a simple 1-2-3-4 rating scale:

1. Never
2. Some of the time
3. Most of the time
4. Always

For your FB% you simply rate your percentage of feedback in each of the drills:

1. 0-25%
2. 25-50%
3. 50-75%
4. 75-100%

Circle where you would rate yourself in each category.

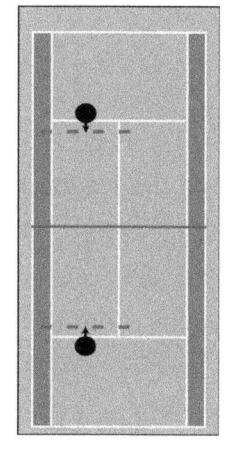

Drill 1

How successfully did you?		
Visualize Window	**Defend Window**	**FB%**
1 2 3 4	1 2 3 4	1 2 3 4

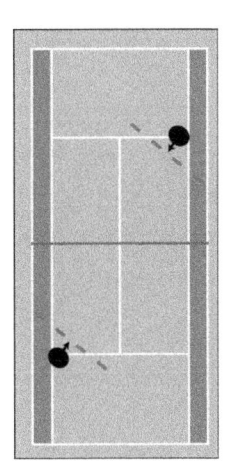

Drill 2

How successfully did you?		
Visualize Window	**Defend Window**	**FB%**
1 2 3 4	1 2 3 4	1 2 3 4

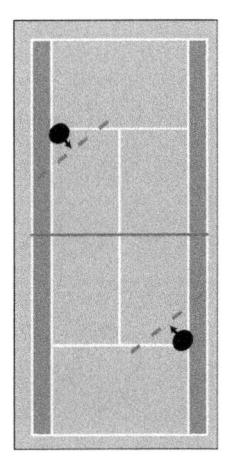

Drill 3

How successfully did you?		
Visualize Window	**Defend Window**	**FB%**
1 2 3 4	1 2 3 4	1 2 3 4

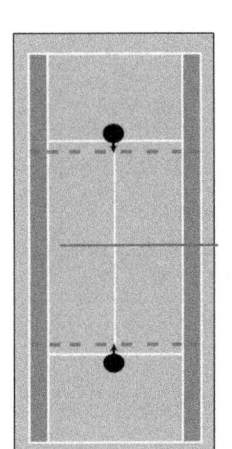

Drill 4

How successfully did you?		
Visualize Window	**Defend Window**	**FB%**
1 2 3 4	1 2 3 4	1 2 3 4

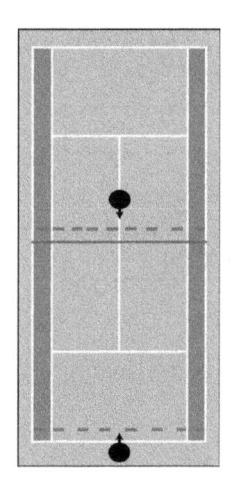

Drill 5

How successfully did you?		
Visualize Window	**Defend Window**	**FB%**
1 2 3 4	1 2 3 4	1 2 3 4

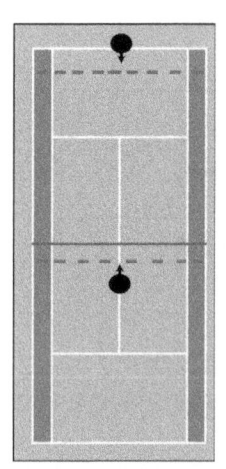

Drill 6

How successfully did you?		
Visualize Window	**Defend Window**	**FB%**
1 2 3 4	1 2 3 4	1 2 3 4

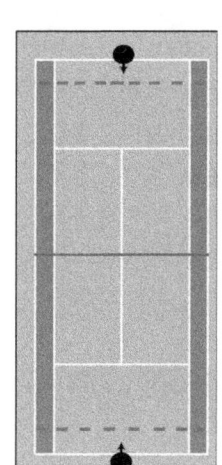

Drill 7

How successfully did you?		
Visualize Window	**Defend Window**	**FB%**
1 2 3 4	1 2 3 4	1 2 3 4

When you have reached the point in each of these drills where you score 3s and 4s in every category, then you are ready to move to the Second Step. If your scores are 2s and 1s, then you should continue with the drills that are the hardest for you until your can raise your score to 3s and 4s in each category. You are not trying to speed through these drills. You are trying to experience the zone in the different depths of the court. If you are not experiencing the zone, then you are probably trying to hit the ball over the net (create an outcome) rather than defend your imaginary window and stay in the process.

Take your time, enjoy being in the zone, and when you are ready, move to the Second Step.

Good luck on your journey.

Chapter 2: A Different Set of Fundamentals

"It seems essential, in relationships and all tasks that we concentrate only on what is most significant and important."
— Soren Kierkegaard

Key Subjects
2.1: The Contact Sequence
2.2: The Contact Zone
2.3: The Three Faces of Timing
2.4: The Primary Contact Point
2.5: The Contact Quadrants
2.6: How To Objectively Measure Your Timing

2.1: The Contact Sequence

We've all been told that we must focus on the ball in order to play the game of tennis. It is the cardinal rule of the game, the one rule that cannot be broken:

- You *must* focus on the ball.
- You *must* concentrate on the ball.
- The *BALL* matters!

The ball may very well be what matters when it comes to playing tennis in the norm, but when it comes to playing tennis in the zone, here's a different perspective: *CONTACT* matters!

The ball matters only in that it is a part of the contact event. The other part of the contact event that matters is your racquet. The ball and your racquet matter only because they come together at a single point in space and time to create what really matters, and what really matters is CONTACT.

Physically, all contact sports including tennis are based on a simple Contact Sequence that looks like this: First comes the Movement of the ball (Mvt), followed by your Countermovement to intercept the ball with your racquet (Cmvt), ending in either a positive or negative Contact Event.

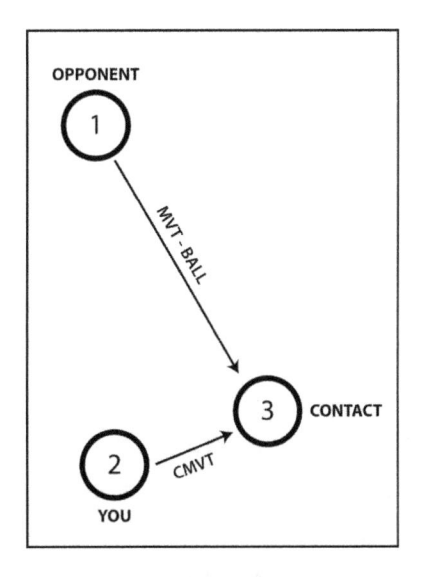

Mvt ⟶ Cmvt ⟶ Contact

1 ⟶ 2 ⟶ 3

Create positive contact and you perpetuate the rally. You remain in the point. Create negative contact through either a forced or unforced error and you end the rally. You lose the point.

Given the basic physical elements of the contact sequence, it's apparent that the only way to win a match is through the continuous creation of positive contact.

If you stand back from the game a short distance and look at the core events that occur on the tennis court, you can see that tennis involves a relationship in space and time between the movement of the ball, your countermovement, and contact. Whatever stroke you are using, whether it's a forehand or a backhand, a volley or half-volley, that stroke is a countermovement created by your sensorimotor operating system, and this countermovement must form a positive relationship in space and time with the movement of the ball in order to create positive contact.

The traditional approach to creating positive contact is to form a positive relationship between your stroke and the ball. If your stroke forms a positive relationship in space and time with the movement of the ball, you end up creating positive contact.

Here's another way to look at the contact sequence relationship. If your stroke forms a positive relationship in space and time with the contact point, you also end up creating positive contact.

In order to achieve this positive relationship with your *contact point*, you start by forming a positive relationship with your *contact zone*. This means that instead of trying to control the ball with your strokes, you try to control your contact zone with your strokes.

The Second Step is about learning to control your contact zone and, in so doing, learning to control the contact point.

2.2: The Contact Zone

In order to control your contact zone, you must first be able to focus on your contact zone, and then you must be able to stay focused on your contact zone. Learning to fix your focus on your contact zone is what the First Step is about. By visualizing an imaginary window in front of you at all times, you are fixing your focus on your contact zone. And by defending your imaginary window from oncoming balls, you are using your strokes to control your contact zone and to continuously create a contact event at the contact point on your imaginary window.

When I first started going into the zone and studying it from the inside, I found that there was more to this concept of visualizing and defending an imaginary window than first meets the eye. As I got more comfortable with fixing my focus on my contact zone, I found that along with becoming more aware of my positive contact, I was also becoming more aware of my negative contact. Even when I was in the zone, I found myself making negative contact at times, and the more I observed this happening in a completely non-judgmental way, the more I realized that there were similarities in the location of my negative contact events relative to my window. So I decided to give my contact zone more depth and definition. I did this by adding another imaginary window. This second window, instead of being arm's length in front of me, was right against my body, as if I was standing with my nose directly against a large windowpane.

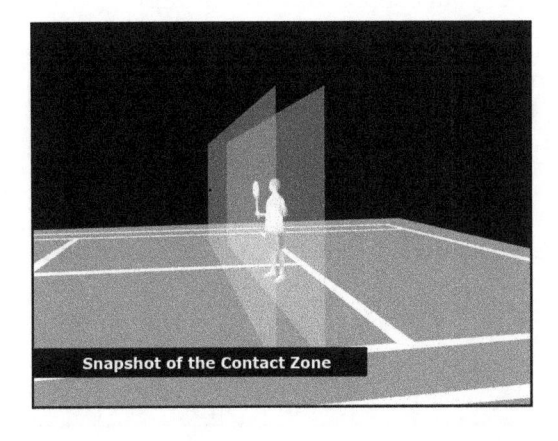

Snapshot of the Contact Zone

34 | Welcome To The Zone

These two imaginary windows represent the full height, width, and depth of your contact zone. The front window represents the front side of your contact zone, while the back window represents the back side of your contact zone. This gives you a 3-dimensional visual representation of what your contact zone looks like, and it also gives you an objective way to measure the difference between good and bad timing.

By assigning numbers to the different depths of the contact zone, you can objectively measure the timing of your strokes.

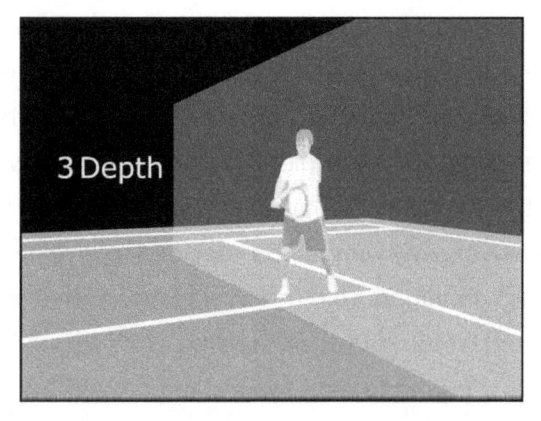

The front side of your contact zone is a 3-Depth

The middle of your contact zone is a 2-Depth

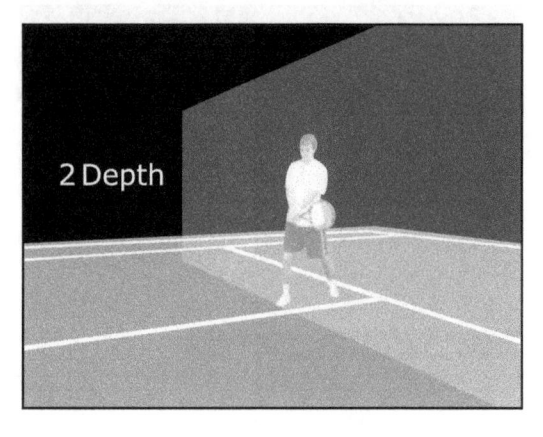

Chapter 2: A Different Set of Fundamentals | 35

The backside of your contact zone is a 1-Depth

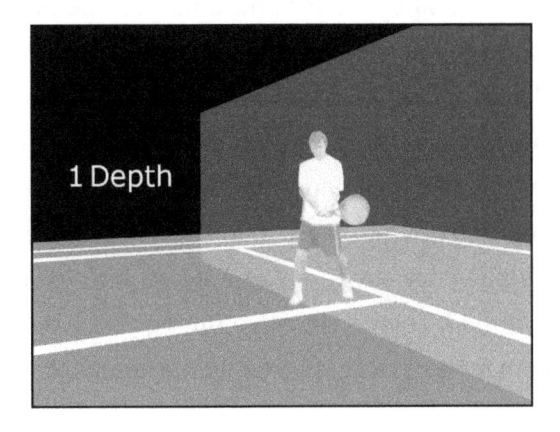

1 Depth

To see things even more clearly, I drew this up on paper using a very simple diagram and the basic elements of every contact sequence: Movement, Countermovement, Contact, and my Contact Zone.

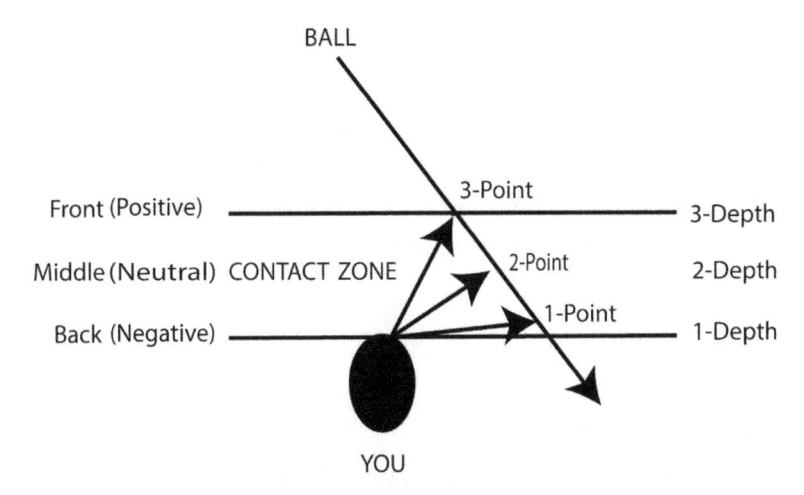

BALL

Front (Positive) — 3-Point — 3-Depth
Middle (Neutral) CONTACT ZONE 2-Point 2-Depth
Back (Negative) — 1-Point — 1-Depth

YOU

2.3: The Three Faces of Timing

Every ball that enters your contact zone can be contacted at one of these three depths, and the depth at which you make contact gives you an objective look at your timing relative to your contact zone.

Contact at a 3-Depth means your stroke was in full control of the contact zone; the ball never penetrated the contact zone. Contact occurred at the exact point in space and time that the ball first entered your contact zone, the 3-Point. Contact at the 3-Point is Positive Timing.

If you make contact at a 2-Depth, then the ball controlled the positive half of the contact zone and your stroke controlled the negative half. Contact at the 2-Point is Neutral Timing.

Contact at a 1-Depth means the ball was in complete control of the contact zone while your stroke never entered into your own contact zone. Contact at the 1-Point is Negative Timing.

This diagram made is easier to explain the complexities of timing to my students:

Contact at a 3-Depth = Positive Timing
Contact at a 2-Depth = Neutral Timing
Contact at a 1-Depth = Negative Timing

I started asking my students who had become comfortable with visualizing and defending their imaginary window to start including a second window in their learning process and to start calling their depth of contact. I immediately started hearing things like:

"That's a three!"
"That was a two."
"Oops! That's a one."
"Yes, that's a three! Three, three, two, three..."

My students began correcting their own timing by objectively measuring their contact locations and then changing locations when they saw negative timing patterns. And as they started correcting their timing, something else started to happen. Their strokes started working better and they started creating positive contact more consistently. I didn't have to do anything! They were doing it all. I simply confirmed their measurements. If they were consistently making contact at a 2-Depth, I asked them to observe what happens when they made contact at a 3-Depth. It didn't take long before they started making contact at their 3-Point, and the positive timing of their strokes resulted in positive contact. With very little instruction from me, they started making shots they were missing earlier in the lesson. By fixing their negative timing, the *parts* of their strokes were starting to come together, resulting in a *whole* stroke that worked, and they were fixing their strokes without any professional wizardry from me.

As I watched them improve, my entire teaching philosophy was being reshaped. I had always prided myself in fixing the parts of a stroke, but here I was, saying nothing and watching as my students fixed what was wrong with their strokes without any instruction from me. I had to bite my tongue to keep from interfering with the learning curve. The less I said, the more they learned for themselves, and the more they learned for themselves, the more they retained. I was teaching less and they were learning more. Go figure.

2.4: The Primary Contact Point

I soon realized that when I made contact at a 3-Depth (the 3-Point), I was creating contact at the exact point the ball first entered my contact zone. I also realized something else. When I created contact at the 3-Point, I seldom missed a shot.

I started thinking of the 3-Point as the *Primary Contact Point* because it was the point at which the ball first entered the space and time of my contact zone. It was also the earliest point at which I could comfortably contact the ball. Plus, when I made contact at the 3-Point, the ball started back in my opponent's direction sooner than if I made contact at the

2-Point or the 1-Point. That fact, plus the fact that I rarely missed when I created contact at the 3-Point, led me to believe that the 3-Point was not only the Primary Contact Point, but, for me, it was also the Optimum Contact Point for every ball entering my contact zone.

A further indication of this was that when my students started creating contact at the 3-Point in their contact zones, they, too, seldom missed a shot. And it didn't matter at what level they played – beginner or advanced. The change was not caused by any big difference in the technique of their strokes, but rather in the consistency of the timing of their strokes.

When they made contact at the 3-Point, one thing was certain: any stroke they used, whatever it looked like technically, took exactly the same amount of time to get to their front window as it took the movement of the ball to get to their front window. No matter how you cut that description, you always end up with a perfect relationship in time between movement and countermovement. You always end up with positive timing.

Lately, the more I teach, the less I say. My lessons are much quieter than they used to be, at least on my part. Mostly what you hear is the constant verbal feedback of students as they observe and objectively measure their own performance. I have found that as long as players are actively engaged in the feedback process there is nothing I can say or do that can make the learning process go any faster. The best thing I can do is shut up and stay out of the way of their learning.

When players reach a point where they are fairly comfortable with focusing on their contact zone, they are ready for the Second Step. Hopefully, you have reached that point by now through practicing visualizing and defending your imaginary window. If so, then you are ready for the next step. But before you go into the Second Step, there is one further refinement to your contact zone that needs to be made.

2.5: The Contact Quadrants

Divide your contact zone into four quadrants by drawing an imaginary vertical line down the center of your window from top to bottom and a horizontal line across the width of your window at shoulder height. This divides your contact zone into four contact quadrants: High-Left, High-Right, Low-Left, and Low-right. (See graphic and diagram below)

CONTACT QUADRANTS

HIGH LEFT (HL)	HIGH RIGHT (HR)
LOW LEFT (LL)	LOW RIGHT (LR)

No matter where you happen to be on the court when your opponent hits the ball, it will generally enter your contact zone in one of these contact quadrants. The Second Step is about observing exactly where contact occurs in your contact quadrants as you move through the various depths of the court from backcourt to midcourt to forecourt.

For instance, when you are in the backcourt, you might observe that contact in your low-right quadrant occurs at a 3-Depth. But in the midcourt and forecourt contact might be occurring more often at a 2-Depth or a 1-Depth. If this is the case, then the timing in your low-right quadrant in the backcourt is positive, but in the midcourt and forecourt the timing in your low-right quadrant is neutral to negative.

In the Second Step the objective is to call your contact depth on every shot you make, in every area of the court, and in all quadrants of your contact zone. The objective is straightforward: call your depth of contact every time you hit the ball. Was it a 3-Depth, a 2-Depth, or a 1-Depth? 3, 2, or 1? You call it. And call it out loud: Immediate verbal feedback.

You will find that the Second Step is not as easy as it sounds. It requires that you not only focus on your contact zone, but that you focus on the location of every contact event. Give it a try. Call your depth of contact.

2.6: How To Objectively Measure Your Timing

Variable Timing

As you practice the Second Step, you will probably find that your contact depth changes, which means your timing is a variable. Variable timing is the first observation most players make when they start calling their contact depth. Even top level players find that their timing varies, more so than they would like to think. By calling your contact depth you will get an honest look at your timing in the different quadrants of your contact zone and at the different depths of the court.

If you observe variable timing in your game, it doesn't mean that your strokes are bad. It just means that your timing is inconsistent, and inconsistent timing leads to inconsistent contact. Good technique with inconsistent timing produces unreliable results, and you end up blaming it on a technical error. In part, you are right. In part, you are wrong. The technical error might not have occurred if the timing error had not occurred. But you won't know that as long as you have variable timing. The trick to seeing your technique's true potential is to observe your technique when it is perfectly timed.

Perfect Timing

Have you ever wondered what it would be like to have perfect timing? What would your strokes feel like if they were always positively timed? If you've been observing your contact depth in the Second Step, then you are aware of what variable timing feels like. It's the norm for most tennis players.

The next exercise in the Second Step is to observe your game when every contact event you create is perfectly timed. How do you do that? By contacting every ball at the Primary Contact Point, the 3-Point, no matter what you have to do with your strokes.

Here's how:

With your practice partner, rally the ball back and forth with the objective of creating contact at the 3-Point no matter where you are on the court and no matter where the ball enters your contact quadrants.

Once again, the objective is not to hit the ball back over the net using some preconceived notion of what your strokes should look like or what type of stroke you should be using as you move around on the court. Instead, trust your stroking intuition and concentrate only on the timing of your contact. Concentrate only on the creation of contact at your front window, contact at the 3-Point.

Every ball, every quadrant, every area of the court, just create contact at the 3-Point. Remember that your objective is not to hit the ball back over the net every time. Rather, your objective is to experience what perfect timing feels like. And you achieve this by consistently creating contact at the 3-Point, the Primary Contact Point.

This exercise in perfect timing requires you to let go of a major learning block: the need to succeed. In order to see what it's like to have perfect timing, you have to let go of the notion that success is only achieved if the ball goes back over the net. Once you get used to creating contact at the 3-Point, you will find that you are also starting to create positive contact more consistently. The more you can control the positive half of your contact zone, the more you will start to get the results your desire, and you'll be getting those results without trying to make them happen.

* * *

In my own journey with the zone, "getting 3's" became the next logical step after I could call my depth of contact. When I teach my workshops, I use the same steps. Once you get past the initial confusion of focusing on your contact zone instead of the ball, you can start observing your contact exactly when and where it happens by calling your depth of contact.

At this point, you will get an honest look at your own timing by observing your contact depth on every stroke. Some players are amazed at the fact that their timing varies so much from one area of the court to another and from one quadrant to another. It shocks them to actually realize the truth about their game. I had never before looked at tennis from the perspective of how my game related to my contact zone. But this perspective actually made the game easier to play. As I moved my contact forward to a consistent 3-Depth, I sensed the parts of my game coming together into a unified whole.

As a teacher I found that this perspective could be used with every tennis player I taught as well as every player I watched, no matter what his or her level of play. Beginners and professionals alike have contact zones, and every player's strokes form a relationship with their contact zone. Better players form a more consistent relationship with the positive half of their contact zone, while less accomplished players form a more consistent relationship with the negative half of their contact zone.

See for yourself the next time you watch a match played at the 2.5

to 3.5 levels. You will see that the majority of contact events occur at the 1 and 2 Depths in the player's contact zone. If that player has a particularly strong stroke, say a strong forehand, you'll notice that the stroke creates contact at or between the 2 and 3 Depths in the forehand quadrants. This is contact in the positive half of the contact zone.

If the same player has a weak backhand, then chances are pretty good that contact in the backhand quadrants occurs at or between the 2 and 1 Depths. This is contact in the negative half of the contact zone.

Then watch a professional match and you will notice that no matter where they are located on the court, the majority of contact in all quadrants occurs at 2's and 3's. Simply put, the pros are not only better because they have sound technique; they are also better because their technique is almost always positively timed.

Over the years they spend on the practice court, professional tennis players have developed strokes that form a positive relationship with their contact zone. Perhaps they know about this relationship, perhaps not. The point is that the pros have developed this relationship with their contact zone to a higher degree than most of the rest of us. Which is why they get paid to play tennis and the rest of us don't.

If you don't spend six hours a day on the court, then it might serve you well to take an honest look at how your overall game relates to your contact zone. Once you see for yourself how your game relates to your contact zone, you are ready to make the changes necessary to correct any relational problems you might have observed.

Everybody wants to perform at a higher level when they go out to play, but that won't happen if your game is forming a negative relationship with your contact zone. Only when your whole game starts forming a relationship with the positive half of your contact zone will you reach a higher level of performance. This doesn't mean you'll get invited to Wimbledon, but you might get invited to play doubles more often.

THE SECOND STEP

1. Call your depth of contact: 3, 2, or 1.
2. Play a game of "getting 3s." See how many 3's you can hit in a row.
3. Use verbal feedback.

Here are some of the flow components you will notice during the Second Step:

Increased Visual Awareness.

By keeping your eyes focused on your contact zone, you will experience an increased visual awareness of everything that happens on the court. Not only will you be peripherally aware of your practice partner hitting the ball over the net, you will also be peripherally aware of the ball coming toward your contact zone, while being acutely aware of the contact event. This increased visual awareness is one of the components of flow.

Total Concentration. As you call your depth of contact, you will notice that you are totally concentrating on the task at hand. Total concentration is a flow component.

Unambiguous Feedback. The 3-2-1 verbal feedback you are using when you call your depth of contact is immediate and unambiguous feedback, another flow component.

Clear Goals. Once again, your objective is not to hit the ball over the net, but rather to call your depth of contact, a clear goal and another of the flow components.

Chapter 2: A Different Set of Fundamentals | 45

Second Step Feedback Page
Measuring Your Timing

MC to MC

(HL)	(HR)
(LL)	(LR)

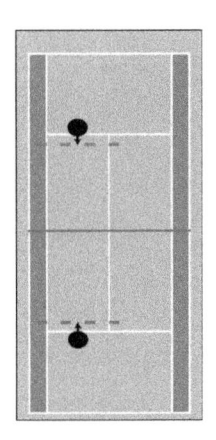

FC to BC

(HL)	(HR)
(LL)	(LR)

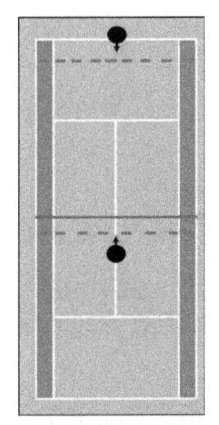

BC to BC

(HL)	(HR)
(LL)	(LR)

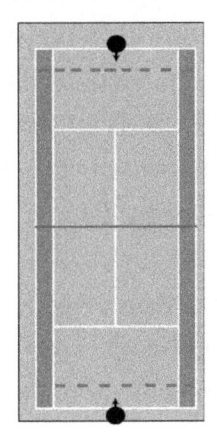

Chapter 3: Fixing Your Focus

"If you know how to focus, unfocus."
— Carlos Castaneda

Key Subjects
3.1: Fixed Focus and the Zone
3.2: Serial Mode and Parallel Mode
3.3: Focused Eyes – Focused Mind
3.4: A Visual Analogy
3.5: Two Opposing Visual Strategies

3.1: Fixed Focus and the Zone

Each step is based on fixing your visual and mental focus on your contact zone. This started with the First Step when you visualized and defended your imaginary window. The act of visualizing a window in front of you literally fixes the focus of your eyes on your contact zone.

In the Second Step, "calling your depth of contact" and "getting 3's" are exercises that require a fixed-focus on your contact zone. It's hard to call your depth of contact if you are not focused on your contact zone, and even harder to make contact at the 3-Point.

Each step builds on your ability to fix and maintain your visual and mental focus on your contact zone. The reason this is important is that a Fixed-Depth of Focus Input Pattern is the visual input pattern underlying tennis in the zone.

While the traditional method of focusing on the ball might sound like the most logical way to use your eyes in a fast-moving ball sport such as tennis; focusing on the ball is a Variable-Depth of Focus Input Pattern, the visual input pattern underlying tennis in the norm.

Variable-Depth of Focus = Tennis in the Norm
Fixed-Depth of Focus = Tennis in the Zone

3.2: Serial Mode and Parallel Mode

As a tennis player you have two performance states: your normal performance state and your peak performance state. Your normal performance state is governed by a sensorimotor operating mode called a Serial Operating Mode. Your peak performance state, however, is governed by a much more efficient and accurate operating mode called a Parallel Operating Mode.

You don't play better tennis because you are in the zone; you play better tennis because when you are in the zone your sensorimotor operating system is functioning in its most efficient and accurate operating mode, a Parallel Mode. The increased efficiency and accuracy of your Parallel Mode is the cause of your higher level of performance.

Making the switch from your Serial Mode to your Parallel Mode is a system dynamics approach to playing tennis in the zone and it's what the Parallel Mode Process is all about. You don't try to create the zone experience by synthesizing the various behavioral components of flow. Instead, you create the zone experience by switching to the underlying system dynamics of the zone, the system dynamics of a Parallel Mode.

In tennis, your sensorimotor operating system functions as an Input/ Processing/Output (IPO) system that must interface with the action on the tennis court. To interface with this action, your eyes input visual information to your brain about the action in your visual field; your brain then processes and integrates that visual information and outputs relative motor information to your body which creates the countermovement you make in response to the action in your visual field. This is basic stimulus-response.

When I learned to play tennis, I was taught to use my IPO system in a very specific way that was characterized by a specific visual input pattern that always involved focusing on the ball. But the more I studied the zone from the inside, the more apparent it became to me that I was using my visual system in a completely different input pattern. I was still inputting visual information to my brain about the action taking place on the tennis court, but I wasn't doing it in the traditional method of "watching the ball." I was not focusing my eyes on the ball any more. Instead, I was fixing the focus of my eyes (and my mind) on my contact zone, my imaginary window, and by simply looking along the surface of this imaginary window, I was able to locate the point the ball first entered my contact zone – the Primary Contact Point.

I found that locating the Primary Contact Point, or, as I called it, the 3-Point, was a much easier way for me to use my eyes than trying to keep a fast-moving tennis ball in focus as it flew rapidly back and forth across the net.

Over the past four decades people have called me some rather colorful names when I told them they didn't have to focus on the ball to play tennis. But the truth is: keeping the ball in focus is impossible at the high speeds we see in tennis. What really happens when you try to keep the ball in focus is that you take little snapshots of the ball at different fixation points along its flight line.

The problem with this seemingly logical method of using your eyes is that by the time you have the ball in focus at one fixation point, it's not there anymore. So your brain is constantly receiving inaccurate visual information about the true location of the ball. Inaccurate visual input invariably leads to inaccurate motor output, and inaccurate motor output manifests itself as negative timing.

According to Dr. William Hines, past team ophthalmologist for the Denver Broncos and Colorado Avalanche and a leading authority in sports vision, the thinking about watching the ball has changed over the years:

> *"We used to think that the only way to use your eyes in tennis or baseball or any fast-moving ball sport was to focus on the object of movement at different points along its flight path. We knew that this serial input method was not very efficient, but there was nothing else available. Then, in the mid-70's research was being done in what we call 'parallel processing.' Research showed that when athletes went into a parallel processing mode, they experienced the slow-motion seeing and quicker reaction times associated with playing in the zone.*
>
> *When I met Scott and he showed me what he was doing with playing tennis in the zone, I knew immediately that he had discovered the input pattern that engages your system in a parallel processing mode. And the reason I knew it immediately was because I went immediately into the zone myself when I switched from a Variable-Depth of Focus visual pattern to a Fixed-Depth of Focus visual pattern.*
>
> *This is it! I said. This is what we've been looking for!"*
> (personal communication, June, 1998)

As a tennis player, you are also a sensorimotor operating system and you have a choice of which input mode you use when you play tennis or any other fast-moving ball sport. The input mode you choose directly affects the processing and output modes in which your operating system performs.

(Serial Input →Serial Processing →Serial Output) = Serial Operating Mode)
(Parallel Input→Parallel Processing→Parallel Output) = Parallel Operating Mode)

Given the choice of performing on the tennis court in your Serial Mode or your Parallel Mode, which would you choose? Your Serial Mode will give you your normal performance state and your normal behavioral state, and for many players that's good enough. Normal is as far as they want to take it. No risk, no stepping outside their comfort zone, nothing behaviorally unusual. But for others, normal is not enough. They want more. They want to experience their peak performance state. For them, the choice is easy. They choose to perform in their Parallel Mode. They choose to play tennis in the zone.

But here's the catch – and there is a catch. In order to perform in your Parallel Mode, you have to detach from your Serial Mode, which means you have to detach from your normal visual behavior.

Simply put, in order to play tennis in the zone, you have to change the way you use your eyes on the tennis court. You have to stop focusing on the ball and start focusing on your contact zone.

It's that simple and it's that difficult at the same time. Understanding the visual change is the easy part. But as you will see, focusing on your contact zone can be as easy or as hard as you want to make it.

3.3: Focused Eyes – Focused Mind

I can remember every coach I ever had screaming at the top of his lungs, usually red-faced and rigid, words to this effect:

"Watch the ball, stupid!"
"Concentrate on the ball, you idiot!"
"You have to focus on the ball, dummy!"

Detect a pattern? We've all been subjected to variations of this common visual theme, and while watching the ball sounds like the right thing to do and seems like the only natural way to use your eyes in tennis, it is, in fact, what keeps you in your normal performance state.

Watching the ball literally locks you into your Serial Operating Mode and, in so doing, locks you into your normal behavioral state. While your Serial Mode with its attendant behavioral state is not a bad operating mode for tennis, it is not your highest-order operating mode, nor is it your highest-order behavioral state.

To get to your peak performance state you have to change both your operating mode and your behavioral state. The two go together, and it's important to understand that you can't have the higher-order behavioral state of flow while you are in your Serial Mode. It just won't happen. Nor can you operate in a Parallel Mode and expect to experience your normal behavioral state. That won't happen either.

This is where players get mixed up when they first learn how to play tennis in the zone. They make the operational change to their Parallel Mode easily enough by changing the way they use their eyes. And for a time, they experience the higher-order behavioral state of flow.

Then something always happens... always. They start thinking about what they are doing rather than just doing it, and by thinking about it, by judging it, by analyzing it, they return to their normal behavioral state, which simultaneously takes them out of their Parallel Mode and out of the zone.

It's just a matter of time before this happens to everyone who learns how to play tennis in the zone. It's like a focal meltdown. If you have been going through the steps, you will have experienced exactly what I am talking about. You will have experienced both the efficiency and accuracy of your operating system performing in its Parallel Mode, and you will have experienced the higher-order behavioral state of flow.

You will also have experienced the meltdown. When you start thinking about what you are doing or when you try to make sense out of the zone, you suddenly realize that you are no longer in the zone. It sneaks up on you at first, eluding detection until its too late and you suddenly realize you are no longer in the zone. Expect this to happen because it will.

Guaranteed.

The purpose of the Third Step is to show you how and why this meltdown occurs and how to prevent it from happening in the future. You see, getting into the zone is easy. All you have to do is switch to your Parallel Mode. Staying in the zone is the tricky part. To maintain the zone you must not interfere with this higher-order behavioral state of flow. You must not disturb the flow state by thinking about it, by analyzing it, by judging it, or by focusing on the results of your performance.

You maintain the zone:

- By detaching from all of your sequential, Serial Mode thinking.
- By detaching from thinking about what you are doing.
- By detaching from analyzing how you are doing it.
- By detaching from judgment and results.

In short, you can't focus your eyes the same way as normal, nor can you focus your mind the same way as normal.

The challenge is not with intellectually understanding this concept of detached awareness. It's been around for centuries. The problem lies in knowing on what to focus your eyes and your mind if you are not focusing in your normal manner. If you are not supposed to focus your eyes or mind on anything that's happening on the court, then what are you supposed to focus on – nothing?

Bingo!

That's exactly what you focus on – nothing. You attach your focus to nothing. Focusing on nothing is the most logical way to keep from focusing on something, such as:

- The ball
- The results of your shot
- What your opponent is doing
- What you are doing

Once you start focusing on any of the people, places or objects on which you normally focus, you will immediately return to your Serial Mode.

Hello, normal performance state.

Goodbye, zone.

By focusing on nothing, you remain non-judgmental, objectively detached from everything. You still see everything; you're just not focused on any of it. Chances are pretty good that this visual arrangement is not what you are used to doing either focally or behaviorally. So, don't expect to perfect this process immediately. Focusing on nothing is the exact opposite of focusing on something. Give it a little time. Control of your focus is not something you master in the same way you master your backhand. Although mastering one will certainly help you master the other.

So, how do you focus on nothing?

Think about this. On what are you focused when you are focused on your contact zone?

When I first noticed that I was focusing on my contact zone instead of the ball, I was faced with a dilemma. I knew I was focusing on the predefined space of my contact zone, but I also knew there was nothing there on which to focus. So I was focused on something that was simultaneously nothing – "no-thing". There's a paradox for you!

My dilemma was that focusing on no-thing – my contact zone – sounded totally unacceptable as a visual strategy, but it was working much better for me than the traditional visual strategy of focusing on something – the ball.

For me, the choice was easy. I went with what worked the best. But I knew I would have to explain the difference between the normal visual pattern we all grew up with – "watch the ball, stupid!" – and this pattern of focusing on my contact zone that I was becoming more comfortable with every day.

Explaining a Fixed-Depth of Focus input pattern was not as easy as saying "watch the ball" or "focus on the ball." It required an explanation that was analogous to a simple visual scenario.

3.4: A Visual Analogy

Imagine standing arm's length away from a large picture window and looking through the window as a boy throws a snowball at the window. Your visual objective is to have the "SPLAT" of the snowball against your window clearly in focus exactly when and where it happens.

This is the same visual task you have to perform when you are trying to have the contact event between the ball and your racquet clearly in focus when and where it happens in your contact zone.

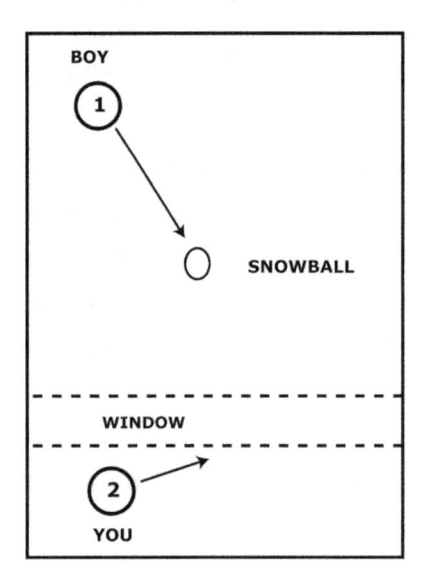

This made pretty good sense to me as an analogy, so I started using it to explain the difference between a Variable-Depth of Focus input pattern (VDF) as a method of locating the SPLAT and a Fixed-Depth of Focus input pattern (FDF) as a method of locating the same SPLAT.

VDF input can most easily be defined as "watch the snowball, stupid."

FDF input can be defined as "focus on the window, then look for the SPLAT."

Both input patterns are logical, if completely different focally. The logic of VDF input states that by keeping the snowball in focus along its entire flight line, you will have the snowball in focus when in contacts the window, therefore the SPLAT will be clearly in focus when and where it happens: a visual process and a visual outcome.

The logic of FDF input states that instead of keeping the snowball in focus, you keep your *window* in focus, then simply look along the surface of the window for the exact point the snowball contacts the window. Since the window is already in focus, when you locate the contact point on your window, you will have the SPLAT clearly in focus when and where it happens: Same visual outcome, different visual process.

The most important difference in these two input patterns lies in the fact that one pattern is much more efficient than the other when it comes to seeing the SPLAT clearly. While watching the snowball (VDF) might seem like the most efficient way to see the SPLAT clearly, it is actually the least efficient of the two visual strategies. VDF input requires refocusing your eyes from far-vision to near-vision in order to see the SPLAT clearly. Refocusing your eyes from far-vision to near-vision is a visual variable.

FDF input is more efficient because you are already *prefocused* on your window/contact zone, and prefocusing on your window/contact zone eliminates this visual variable of refocusing. So, by fixing your focus on your window/contact zone, you are effectively eliminating the refocusing variable by engaging your focus as a constant.

In system dynamics, efficiency is measured by which system accomplishes a given task with the fewest number of system variables. Looking at the dynamics of the human visual system, FDF input is more efficient that VDF input because it accomplishes the task of "seeing the SPLAT clearly," with fewer visual variables.

Prefocusing eliminates refocusing. And when you eliminate the refocusing variable, you not only eliminate a visual variable from the task of locating the contact event, you also eliminate the visual variable that is most responsible for inputting misinformation to the brain about the speed of the ball's movement.

Another important distinction between VDF and FDF input is the difference in visual information your brain is receiving when you focus on the ball versus when you focus on your contact zone. When you focus on the ball, your eyes are inputting information to your brain about the location of the ball in space and time. There is no visual information being input to your brain about the location of your contact zone in space and time. In other words, when you "watch the ball, stupid!" you might see the ball but you won't see your contact zone.

However, when you focus on your contact zone, your eyes are actively inputting information to your brain about the location of your contact zone in space and time. And as you look for the contact point along your imaginary window, you are also actively inputting information to your brain about the location of the ball in space and time. In other words, when you look for the contact point along the surface of your imaginary window, you are inputting information to your brain about the ball and your contact zone simultaneously.

Finally, watching the ball is a *Serial Input Pattern*. You see the ball sequentially from point to point along its flight line. This causes your brain to process in a serial processing mode and output in a serial output mode. The whole serial IPO interface locks your operating system in its normal performance state.

Serial Mode = Serial Interface = Normal Performance State

Prefocusing on your contact zone and looking for the contact point is a *Parallel Input Pattern*. You see the ball and the contact zone simultaneously, *in parallel*. This causes your brain to process in a parallel processing mode and then to output in a parallel output mode. The whole parallel IPO interface locks your operating system in its peak performance state.

Parallel Mode = Parallel Interface = Peak Performance State

When it comes to seeing the SPLAT on your window clearly, "watch the snowball, stupid!" is certainly less efficient and less accurate than looking for the contact point on your window. Given the choice of using an input pattern that locks you into your normal performance state or an input pattern that locks you into your peak performance state, it might just be that "watch the ball, stupid!" is exactly that – stupid.

3.5: Two Opposing Visual Strategies

Variable-Depth of Focus Input (VDF)

Watching the ball is a visual strategy that requires you to continuously refocus your eyes while trying to keep the ball in focus as it moves back and forth across the net. This is a Variable-Depth of Focus input pattern (VDF) – the same as watching the snowball as it comes toward your window - and it is the traditional input pattern employed by tennis players as their default visual strategy.

The logic behind VDF as a visual strategy is this: if you follow the ball closely enough with your eyes, your brain will receive accurate visual information about the speed and direction of the ball's movement. Your brain then assimilates that information and outputs relative motor information to your body about the required speed and direction of your countermovement.

If the visual information your brain receives accurately mirrors the speed and direction of the ball's movement, then your brain will output an accurate motor countermovement.

Accurate Visual Input = Accurate Motor Output

If, however, the visual information your brain receives inaccurately mirrors the speed and direction of the ball's movement, then your brain will output an inaccurate motor countermovement. This inaccurate countermovement takes the form of a stroke that is incorrectly timed. It's the old "garbage in/garbage out" analogy, only on the tennis court it looks like this:

Inaccurate Visual Input = Inaccurate Motor Output

In essence, watching the ball (VDF) is a two-part visual strategy. Part one: focus on the ball when your opponent hits it. (Figure 1) Part two: keep the ball in focus until you hit it. (Figures 2-3)

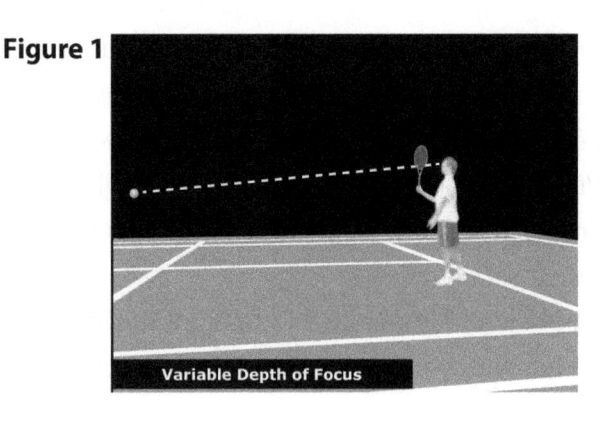

Figure 1

Variable Depth of Focus

Figure 2

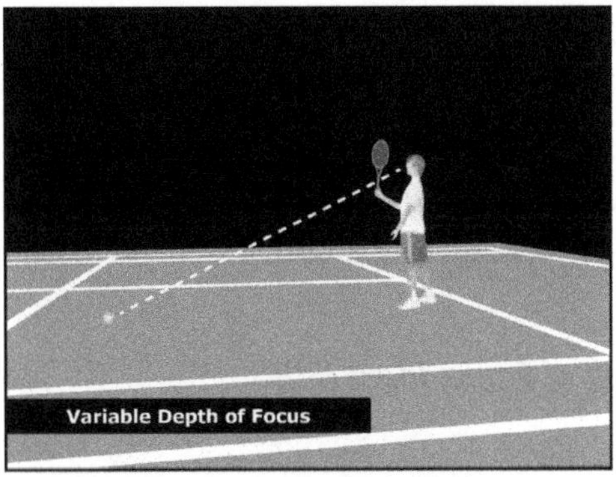

Variable Depth of Focus

Figure 3

Variable Depth of Focus

Part one is the easy part. All you have to do is watch your opponent hit the ball. Part two - keeping the ball in focus until you hit it - is virtually impossible for the human eye at higher speeds, and because the human eye cannot keep the ball in focus at higher speeds, what you end up with is inaccurate visual input.

Garbage in.

Your stroke may continue to form an accurate relationship with the direction of the ball's movement, but because the focus of your eyes can't keep up with the ball, your stroke will form an inaccurate relationship with the ball's speed. End result: you do the right stroke but your timing is off.

Garbage out.

Inaccurate visual input is the primary cause of bad timing, and if you are looking to fix your timing problems by fixing something in your stroking technique, then you are looking in the wrong place. Inaccurate motor output (bad timing) is the last link in the Visual/Cognitive/Motor chain. The problem starts with the first link, the visual input link. So, if you want to fix your timing errors, you have to go to the cause, you have to fix your visual input errors.

Fixed-Depth of Focus Input (FDF)

Like VDF, Fixed-Depth of Focus Input is also a two-part visual strategy. Part one: fix the focus of your eyes on your contact zone by visualizing an imaginary window in front of you. (Figure 4)

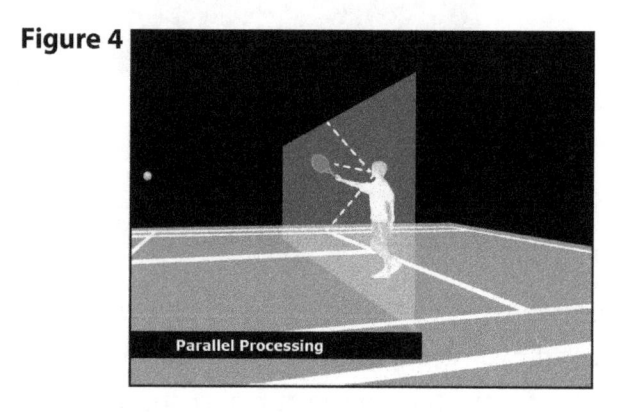

Figure 4

Part two: locate the point the ball contacts the surface of your window. (Figure 5)

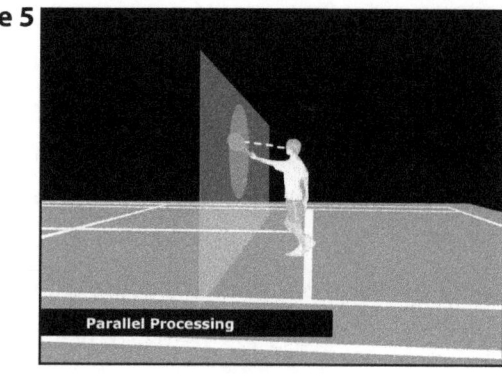

Figure 5

When you locate the point the ball contacts the surface of your imaginary window, you have effectively located the exact point in space and time that the ball first enters your contact zone – the *Primary Contact Point*.

The strategic difference between Variable-Depth of Focus and Fixed-Depth of Focus is that with VDF you use your eyes to input information to your brain about the direction and speed of the ball's movement, but with FDF you use your eyes to input information to your brain about the location in space and time of the Primary Contact Point.

VDF = Direction and Speed of ball's movement (Direction/Speed)
FDF = Location of Primary Contact Point (Time/Space)

One of the first sensations players get when they are learning to locate the contact point along the surface of their imaginary window is the sense of the ball coming into focus as it moves toward their imaginary window, then going out of focus as it moves away from their window. Logically, this is what *should* happen, but you will find that this change of visual awareness takes some getting used to. As competitors, we place so much value on the outcome of our strokes that we naturally want to focus on the ball after we hit it to see whether or not our shots go in.

But when you think about it, if you focus on the ball as it goes back over the net, you immediately come out of FDF input and return to VDF input, which puts you right back into "watching the ball, stupid," the same way you have always watched the ball. Learning to prefocus on your contact zone and then maintain a fixed-focus on your contact zone requires letting go of the outcome of your shots by not focusing on the ball after contact.

You will still "see" the ball as it goes back over the net. It's the fuzzy yellow blur moving away from your contact zone. But because you are mentally and visually focused on your contact zone, you are simultaneously *not* focusing on the ball, *not* concentrating on the ball, and therefore you will *not* become attached to the outcome of your shots.

Fixing your focus on your contact zone causes you to defocus from the ball and thus *automatically* detaches you from the outcome. Defocusing visually from the ball detaches you mentally and emotionally from the outcome.

You will soon find out that letting go of the outcome is not as easy as it sounds. It takes time to learn, but as you become more familiar with focusing on your contact zone, not only will you learn something about visually letting go of the outcome; you will also learn something about mentally and emotionally letting go of the outcome. For some players, this letting go process is the hardest part of playing tennis in the zone.

So, this is FDF input, and as a visual strategy, it is a more efficient way to locate the contact point than watching the ball. More efficient for one very simple reason previously mentioned: the act of prefocusing your eyes on your contact zone eliminates the necessity of refocusing your eyes to your contact zone.

Prefocusing eliminates refocusing.

And when you eliminate the refocusing variable from your visual strategy, you also eliminate the primary cause of bad timing. Moreover, a visual strategy with fewer variables is a more efficient visual strategy at higher speeds. And, remember, the more efficient and accurate your visual input, the more efficient and accurate your motor output.

Accurate Visual Input = Accurate Motor Output

THE THIRD STEP

The Third Step involves an exercise in visual concentration. It starts again at the "T" but your objective is not to simply defend your imaginary window but to visually locate the 3-Point along the surface of your imaginary front window. This exercise specifically trains you to use Fixed-Depth of Focus input (Parallel) rather than using Variable-Depth of Focus input (Serial).

In this exercise, contact between racquet and ball should occur at the 3-Point, and in order to make contact at the 3-Point, you must first locate the 3-Point. That's what the Third Step is about: learning to visually locate the 3-Point on a fixed-focal plane

Learning FDF input takes visual concentration, and concentrating on what you are doing with your eyes is not the same as concentrating on what you are doing with your body. Remember, this is a visual exercise, not a physical exercise. It is designed to train your eyes to locate a specific point along a predefined focal plane. It is not about the results of your contact. In other words, think about your eyes, not your body or your racquet. If you can locate the 3-Point with your eyes, you will definitely be able to hit it with your racquet.

The Third Step is a natural next step from the Second Step, which has the objective of calling your depth of contact – 3, 2 or 1. The difference lies in the fact that the Third Step has a visual objective. Instead of calling the depth at which contact occurs, you are actively using your eyes to locate the exact point at which the ball first enters your contact zone – the 3-Point.

Your immediate feedback is a verbal "yes/no" on whether or not you successfully located the 3-Point with your eyes. Once you are comfortable with this visual exercise from midcourt to midcourt, start to increase your visual depth of field by moving to the backcourt while your partner moves to the forecourt. Eventually, you should both be able to use FDF input from backcourt to backcourt as well as moving throughout the depths of the court.

Remember, your objective is *not* to watch the ball, but rather to keep your eyes focused on your contact zone and look for the point at which the ball first enters your contact zone. That point is the 3-Point. Locate the 3-Point along the surface of your imaginary window, create contact at the 3-Point and do not focus on the outcome. Focus instead on maintaining your fixed-depth of focus. Stay focused on your window.

* * *

Visual concentration requires that you concentrate on what you are doing with your eyes and *not* what you are doing with your body or with your racquet. Think of the Third Step as an exercise in visual signal-sending. You are learning to send visual signals to your brain about the location of the Primary Contact Point. Do not expect it to feel like "watching the ball." It won't.

Locating the contact point along a predefined focal plane is a completely different method of inputting visual information in your visual field. Expect it to feel different. If it does not feel different, you are still watching the ball.

Flow Components and the Third Step

All of the components of flow are present when you are in the zone, but some are more apparent than others. In this exercise, action/awareness merging or the sensation of going on "automatic pilot" is an indicator that you are doing the drill successfully. Simply observe this phenomenon when it happens. It means you are in the zone and using your eyes in an FDF input pattern.

Q: How can I tell what's going on if I don't focus on my opponent or the ball?

A: FDF input is different from VDF input. Your perception of what is going on in front of you will also be different. When you are focused on your imaginary window, you will still "see everything" that is going on in your visual field, but you will be "focused on nothing." You will still be able to see what your opponent is doing, but it will always be out of focus, peripheral. The ball, however, will continue to come into focus as it comes closer to your contact zone.

Third Step Feedback Page

As in the first two steps, the feedback page is all about measuring your improvement in this specific area of the Parallel Mode Process. Specifically, measuring your improvement in making the change from VDF to FDF. By giving yourself objective, yes/no feedback, you will be able to see how well you are doing with FDF.

This step is perhaps the most important in the Parallel Mode Process because it deals directly with what you are doing with your eyes. It is also the most difficult of the steps for the same reason. It deals with what you are doing with your eyes instead of what you are doing with your body.

Playing tennis in the zone is based on playing tennis in a fixed-focus state, so the importance of learning how to use FDF as your primary visual input pattern cannot be overstated. Much of the early zone training is spent with students learning to get comfortable with and improve their ability to use FDF in different competitive situations.

What you are trying to measure in these FDF visual drills is your ability to give verbal "yes/no" feedback on *completing the task* of locating the Primary Contact Point (3-Point) on your imaginary window. Notice that you are NOT giving yourself yes/no feedback on what happens *after* you locate the 3-Point, but rather your feedback involves a yes or a no on locating the 3-Point and, if you do not locate the 3-Point, then identifying your flash-out. (NOTE: flash-outs are any time you lose focus on the Contact Zone. More on flash-outs in Chapter 5).

Remember this: if you did not locate the 3-Point on your imaginary window, then you *did* flash out.

Self-Rating Your Progress

Once again, the three things you are measuring on the Feedback page are:

1. Visualizing an imaginary window in front of you at a comfortable arm's length, and maintaining your visual and mental focus on your contact zone throughout the course of the point. (Fixed Focus State)
2. Locating the point the ball contacts your imaginary window. (Locating the Primary Contact Point)
3. Immediate verbal "yes/no" feedback percentage (FB%).

Your rating system for locating the contact point on your imaginary window (3-Point) in each of the drills is a simple 1-2-3-4 rating scale.

1. Never
2. Some of the time
3. Most of the time
4. Always

For your FB% you simply rate your percentage of feedback in each of the drills.

1. 0-25%
2. 25-50%
3. 50-75%
4. 75-100%

68 | Welcome To The Zone

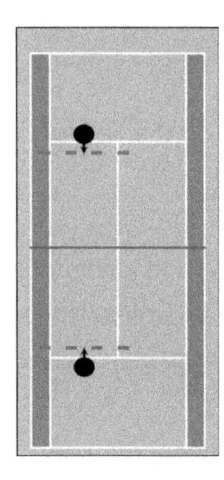

Drill 1

Circle where you would rate yourself in each category.

How successfully did you:		
Maintain Focus	**Locate 3**	**FB%**
1 2 3 4	1 2 3 4	1 2 3 4

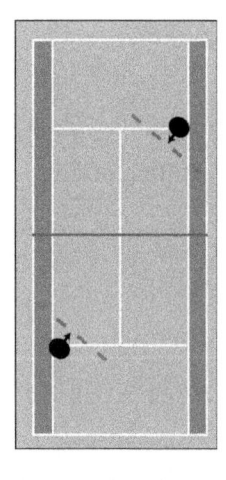

Drill 2

Circle where you would rate yourself in each category.

How successfully did you:		
Maintain Focus	**Locate 3**	**FB%**
1 2 3 4	1 2 3 4	1 2 3 4

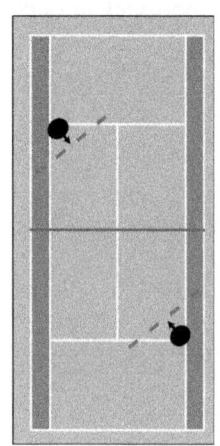

Drill 3

Circle where you would rate yourself in each category.

How successfully did you:		
Maintain Focus	**Locate 3**	**FB%**
1 2 3 4	1 2 3 4	1 2 3 4

Chapter 3: Fixing Your Focus | 69

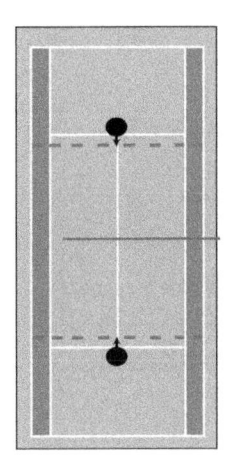

Drill 4

Circle where you would rate yourself in each category.

How successfully did you:		
Maintain Focus	**Locate 3**	**FB%**
1 2 3 4	1 2 3 4	1 2 3 4

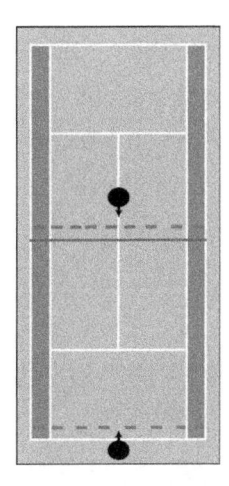

Drill 5

Circle where you would rate yourself in each category.

How successfully did you:		
Maintain Focus	**Locate 3**	**FB%**
1 2 3 4	1 2 3 4	1 2 3 4

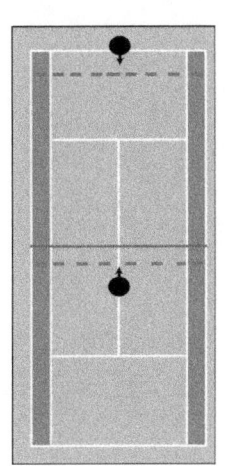

Drill 6

Circle where you would rate yourself in each category.

How successfully did you:		
Maintain Focus	**Locate 3**	**FB%**
1 2 3 4	1 2 3 4	1 2 3 4

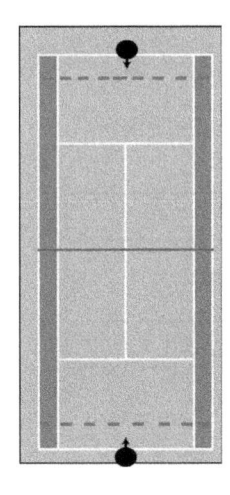

Drill 7

Circle where you would rate yourself in each category.

How successfully did you:		
Maintain Focus	Locate 3	FB%
1 2 3 4	1 2 3 4	1 2 3 4

As always, you are not trying to speed through these drills. You are trying to experience FDF in the different depths of the court. If you are flip-flopping back and forth between FDF and VDF, then you are completely normal. Everybody goes through the same back and forth confusion at first. That's why you do these drills. They are designed to make you consciously aware of whether you are using your eyes in a VDF input pattern or a FDF input pattern.

Take your time, deal with what it takes to make the switch to FDF and learn what it's like to play the game in a fixed focus state.

Chapter 4: Serving in the Zone

Key Subjects

4.1: The Dimensions of the Serving Zone.

4.2: The Serving Sequence.

4.3: The 3-Point on the Serve.

4.4: Calling Your Contact Point on the Serve

4.5: Focusing Your Eyes On the 3-Point

4.6: Alignment at Contact

4.7: Three Basic Serves

4.1: The Dimensions of the Serving Zone

As you stand at the service line imagine that you are standing in a hallway that leads across the net into the service court. This hallway has width: a right side, a center, and a left side (see below).

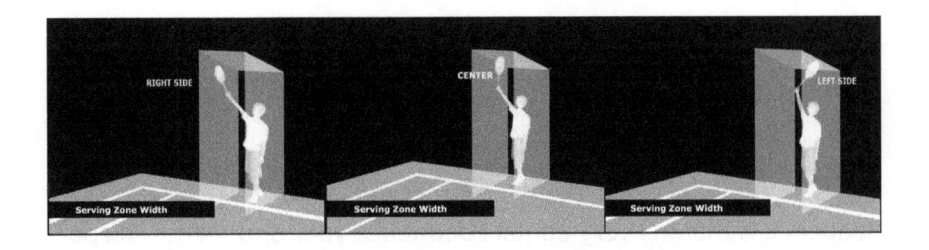

Your serving zone also has height (see below).

And finally, your serving zone also has depth (see below).

What you have now is a picture of a 3-dimensional serving zone, a serving zone with height, width, and depth. If you stretch your tossing arm straight forward into the center of your serving zone and imagine touching a window that extends up as high as you can reach your racquet, you also have a flat surface upon which to measure the vertical alignment of your racquet at contact.

4.2: The Serving Sequence

The only difference between the Contact Sequence and the Serving Sequence is that in every Contact Sequence your opponent is responsible for providing the ball's movement in your direction, while you are only responsible for the countermovement you make to intercept the ball with your racquet.

But in the Serving Sequence, you are responsible for both the movement of the ball as well as your countermovement to intercept the ball with your racquet. This is the only time in tennis when you are in control of both movement and countermovement. The only chance you get to control both the ball and your swing. Yet the serve is perhaps the most difficult of all tennis strokes to master.

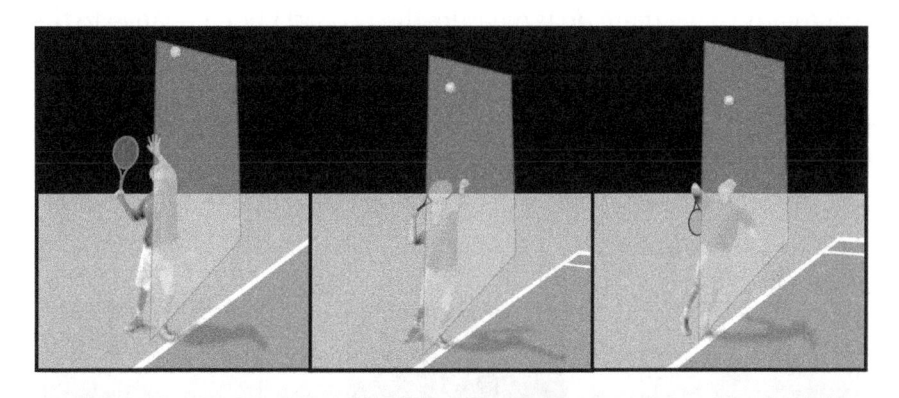

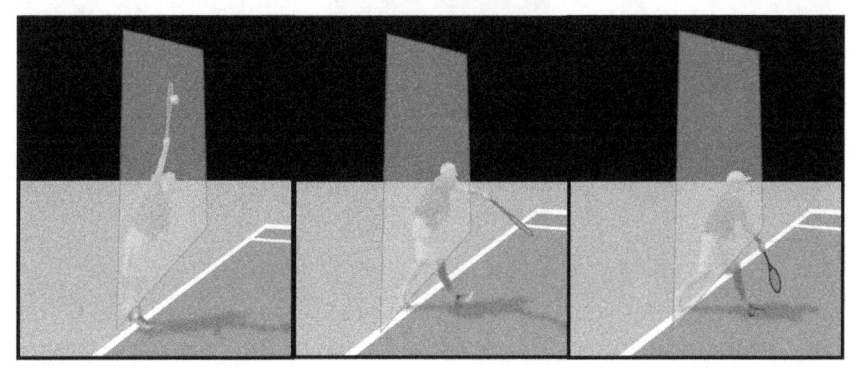

In the earlier steps you learned about using an imaginary window as a representation of your contact zone as well as how to use a predefined depth of contact to measure and improve the timing of your contact. Now you will see how the same concept of an imaginary window can be used to measure and improve your entire Serving Sequence: your toss, your swing, and contact.

4.3: The 3-Point on the Serve.

There are differing opinions about where your contact point should be on your serve, so when I teach players to serve in the zone, one of the first things I have them do is measure their contact point relative to the dimensions of their serving zone. I suggest as a point of contact a point located at a 3-height, 3-depth, and somewhere close to the center of the serving zone.

The photos below show several different views of the 3-Point within a player's serving zone.

In tennis, the Serving Sequence is similar to the Contact Sequence in that it involves the movement of the ball (toss), your countermovement to intercept the ball (swing), and contact, the event of the ball and your swing coming together at a common point in space and time: the Contact Point.

4.4: Calling Your Contact Point on the Serve

Here's the drill: hit ten consecutive serves from the deuce court and try to call your point of contact once you have hit the serve. In other words, rather than just tossing the ball up in the air and hitting a serve, be aware of the exact location of your contact point. Did you make contact at a 3-height? A 3-depth? Was your contact point in the center of your serving zone or too far to the right or left?

Now hit ten consecutive serves from the ad court and continue to call your point of contact. The whole idea of this drill is to become more aware of your contact point relative to your serving zone. It won't take long before you are able to decisively measure and call your points of contact as you serve. This, in itself, is not meant to improve your serve, but to give you a very honest look at where your contact is occurring on your serve.

Once you are able to call the contact point on your serve, you are ready to make corrections in the location of your contact point. The biggest problem I see in serving is not with the player's swing, but rather with the player's toss. Simply put, most recreational players and many open level players have an inconsistent toss, which means they will have an inconsistent contact location as well as an inconsistent time of contact.

In order to have a consistent time and place of contact on your serve, you must first develop a consistent toss, and a consistent toss means a toss that consistently goes to the same location in your serving zone. One location to use as your target location is the junction of a 3-height and 3-depth in the center of your serving zone. I call this the "3-Point."

4.5: Focusing Your Eyes On the 3-Point

One of the main reasons players have trouble tossing consistently to a consistent contact point in their serving zone is that they naturally watch the ball when they toss rather than looking at the target of their toss. Try this easy exercise to see where you are looking on your toss.

Stand approximately arm's length from the fence or the backdrop and reach your racquet as high as you can onto the backdrop (3-Point). Now, using your normal tossing motion, toss the ball to the 3-Point on the backdrop. Repeat the toss five to ten times and then notice what you are looking at with your eyes as you toss the ball. Are you looking at the ball, or are you looking at the target (3-Point) on the backdrop?

Chances are pretty good that you are looking at the target on the backdrop. That's the natural way you use your eyes when you are trying to hit a target with your toss. You look at the target first, and then you toss to the target. You do not look at the ball and then toss it to an unsighted target. Yet that is exactly what most players do when they toss the ball on their serve. First they look across the net at the target of their serve, and then they look at the ball as they toss it into the air above them.

Question: When, in that visual sequence did they locate the target of their toss with their eyes?

Now go back to the service line and hit ten more serves into the deuce court. What are you doing with your eyes when you toss the ball on each serve? Are you using your eyes to target the contact location or are you using your eyes to watch the ball?

The next exercise is to hit ten serves from each court, but instead of watching the ball as you toss it in the air; your objective is to target your 3-Point with your eyes prior to tossing the ball.

This strategy of visually locating your contact point prior to your toss takes getting used to. Normally, you don't think about what you are doing with your eyes when you serve.

Normally, your swing thoughts range anywhere from what you are doing with your feet, to what you are doing with your knees, to what you are doing with your backswing, to where you are aiming your serve. The list is huge, but the one thing that you probably don't think about when you are serving is what you are doing with your eyes. This takes concentration, both mental and visual, so be prepared for an exercise in serving that feels different right from the start.

4.6: Alignment at Contact

One of the biggest mistakes players make when they serve is to think that they can hit the ball down into the service court. For most players, the racquet head must be close to vertical at contact. In other words, you strike the ball with vertical racquet strings and gravity pulls the ball down into the service court.

When I teach people how to serve in the zone, I always use the same concept of an imaginary window located arm's length in front of them in their serving zone. Having an imaginary window in front of you allows you to visualize a *flat surface* for your racquet to contact. For instance, if you were to swing your racquet up and flat against the back curtains or up and flat against the back fence, you would get a visual of what it looks and feels like to have vertical racquet strings at contact.

4.7: Three Basic Serves

The Flat Serve

Remember that your object of contact is the flat surface of your imaginary window, not the round surface of the ball. The ball will be there at the 3-point when your racquet arrives, and if you make contact with the flat surface of your window, you will also be contacting the ball with vertical racquet strings. If you just swing up and contact the round surface of the ball, your strings might not be vertical.

In the ad-court all you do is change the angle of your imaginary window to be perpendicular to the court you are serving into. Then just swing up and flat through the window as it is angled toward the ad-court. Again, if your strings are vertical at contact, your serve should go in.

The Spin Serve

A side-spin or slice serve can also be achieved by using your imaginary window as a guide for both your toss and your swing. Start by positioning your imaginary window directly against your left side and extending up as if you were standing with your left side against a wall.

Your 3-point remains at a 3-height, but you might want to toss the ball to the right side of your hallway at about a 2-depth or even a 1-depth. Experiment with this to find your most comfortable contact "depth" on the side-spin serve. Then it's just a matter of swinging your racquet up along the surface of your imaginary window and across the 3-point and you will impart side-spin on the ball.

The Topspin Serve

Similarly, you can use your imaginary window as a guide for both your toss and your swing on the topspin serve. Personally, I like to toss the ball to a 3-point located on the left side of my hallway at about a 1-depth. Again, find the most comfortable depth of contact for your toss on the topspin serve. For me, contact at a 1-depth or 2-depth on the left side of my hallway is the most comfortable.

To impart topspin on the ball, you simply swing your racquet up along the surface of your window and across the 3-point.

REVIEW

1. Set up your serving zone:
- Visualize a hallway leading to the court you are serving into.
- Visualize a window at arm's length in front of you inside your serving hallway.

2. The toss:
- Locate the 3-point on your imaginary window prior to your toss.
- Toss to the 3-point on your imaginary window.

3. The swing
- Swing up and flat through your imaginary window.
- Make contact at the 3-point (vertical racquet strings).

THE SHORT VERSION
- Look for the 3-point.
- Toss to the 3-point.
- Contact at the 3-point.

PHASE II
Core Concept: Maintaining the Zone

Once you have learned how to get in the zone by choice, not chance, it's time to learn how to maintain and stabilize your peak performance state.

The Parallel Mode Process accomplishes this by maintaining and stabilizing your connection to the present dimension of each successive Contact Sequence in time and space.

Chapter 5: Playing in the Present

"The distinction between past, present and future is only a stubbornly persistent illusion."
— Albert Einstein

Key Subjects
5.1: Connecting to the Present Dimension
5.2: Temporal Location
5.3: The Zone and Time
5.4: Serial and Parallel Interface
5.5: Letting Go of the Past
5.6: Flash-Outs
5.7: Future Focus and Anticipation
5.8: Two Visual Pathways of the Brain
5.9: Heightened Visual Awareness

5.1: Connecting to the Present Dimension

While studying the zone from the inside, I noticed something that had been right in front of me the whole time. It dealt with the basic contact sequence that lies at the heart of the game of tennis. What I noticed was that there was a consistent temporal relationship in every contact sequence: a relationship in time between the three elements of every contact sequence:

Movement -> Countermovement –> Contact

It was a simple observation with profound implications. I had always wondered about the concept of "being in the present." What does that really mean? How do you know if you are really in the present or not? For that matter, if you are *not* playing in the present, then in what temporal dimension are you playing?

I knew one thing for certain: although every contact sequence in tennis has a different look to it (forehand contact sequence, backhand contact sequence, volley contact sequence, etc), *the one thing that never changes is the order in which every contact sequence occurs.*

Every contact sequence always plays itself out the same way. First comes the Movement of the ball (Mvt), second comes my Countermovement (Cmvt) to intercept the ball, and third comes Contact (Cnt), the event that occurs when the ball and my racquet come together at a common point in space and time.

Every contact sequence always looks like this in time:

$$\begin{array}{ccc} \mathbf{Mvt} \rightarrow & \mathbf{Cmvt} \rightarrow & \mathbf{Cnt} \\ 1 \rightarrow & 2 \rightarrow & 3 \\ \mathbf{Ball} \rightarrow & \mathbf{Me} \rightarrow & \mathbf{Contact} \end{array}$$

When I looked at the relationship in time (temporal indexing) of the three elements of the contact sequence, it was apparent that the movement of the ball always occurred *before* my countermovement and contact always occurred *after* my countermovement. In terms of temporal indexing, that meant movement always occurred in my past, and contact would always be in my future until it actually happened.

Then the whole sequence would start all over again, only in my opponent's direction.

Given this temporal relationship, the contact sequence took on a different look:

$$\text{Mvt} \rightarrow \text{Cmvt} \rightarrow \text{Cnt}$$
$$\text{Ball} \rightarrow \text{Me} \rightarrow \text{Contact}$$
$$\text{Past} \rightarrow \text{Present} \rightarrow \text{Future}$$

This simple view of how the elements of the contact sequence related to each other in time was quite a bit different from how the same elements looked in space:

$$\text{Mvt} \rightarrow \text{Cnt} \leftarrow \text{Cmvt}$$
$$\text{Ball} \rightarrow \text{Contact} \leftarrow \text{Me}$$
$$\text{Past} \rightarrow \text{Future} \leftarrow \text{Present}$$

And to understand this better I drew a simple diagram that showed how this contact sequence played out in time in the real-life action of the tennis court:

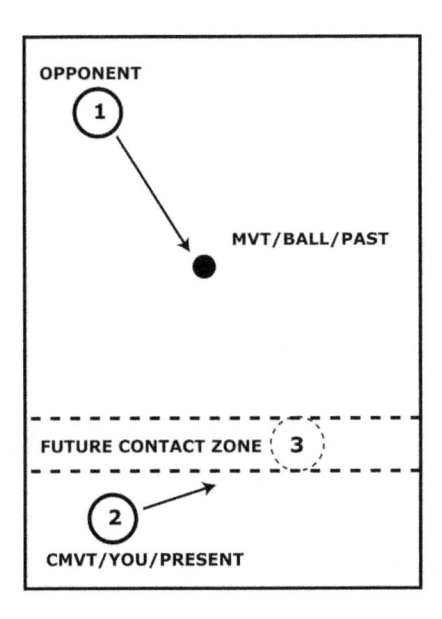

This "simple" diagram found its way to a team of theoretical mathematicians at NORAD in Colorado Springs, Colorado who didn't think it was so simple (but that's another story). What they agreed on was that this diagram represented a sound physical model of the spatial and temporal relativity of the contact sequence, and the more I looked at this model, the more I realized that I was looking at the clues to one of the biggest mysteries in all of sport. The mystery of what it means to be "in the present."

5.2: Temporal Location

You, as Countermovement, are physically located in the present. In front of you, existing simultaneously in your visual field, are both the location of the ball and the location of your contact zone. Relative to you in the present, the ball is temporally located in your past and the contact zone is temporally located in your future.

In other words, your immediate past and your immediate future are alive and well right there in front of your eyes, and how you use your focus will determine the temporal location of your mind. You can choose to focus on the ball, Variable-Depth of Focus, in which case your eyes will be sending your brain temporal information about the past movement of the ball, but they will not be sending your brain any temporal information about the future depth of contact.

What that means is that when you focus on the ball, you are only receiving information about the past relative to you. You are not receiving any information about the future relative to you. That's what you get when you use VDF as your visual input pattern. You get information about the past temporal location of the ball only.

If, however, you use Fixed-Depth of Focus as your visual input pattern and choose to focus on your contact zone, then your eyes will not only be sending your brain temporal information about the future depth of contact, but since you can still see the ball as you look for the contact point along the surface of your imaginary window, your eyes will also be sending your brain temporal information about the past movement of the ball. Moreover, this temporal information about the future depth of contact and the past movement of the ball is being sent to your brain simultaneously. So instead of just receiving information about the past (ball) only, you are receiving information about the past (ball) and the future (Contact Zone) simultaneously.

VDF = temporal information about the past only.
FDF = temporal information about the past and future simultaneously.

What this means in terms of your temporal location when you play tennis is that when you focus on the ball (VDF), your brain is only receiving temporal information about the past dimension of the contact sequence. *Your body might be in the present, but your mind is in the past.*

But when you locate the contact point along a fixed focal plane (FDF), your brain is receiving temporal information about the past and the future dimensions equally and simultaneously. In other word, as you focus on your imaginary window/contact zone and locate the 3-Point, your brain is continuously receiving equal amounts of information about the past and the future dimensions of the contact sequence simultaneously.

Question: What temporal dimension is created when your brain is receiving visual information about the past and the future equally and simultaneously?

Same question - version two: in what temporal dimension are you when you are equally in the past and the future at the same time?

Answer: you are in the present - the third temporal dimension.

When you use FDF as your visual input pattern, both your body and your mind are "in the present."

5.3: The Zone and Time

Being in the present is what playing tennis in the zone, or playing any other sport in the zone, is all about. The underlying temporal dimension of your peak performance state is not the past, is not the future, but rather and equal and simultaneous combination of both. You create the present temporal dimension by combining equal portions of the immediate past and immediate future simultaneously.

But you do not do it by watching the ball. Watching the ball locks you in the past temporal dimension. In fact, watching the ball is the reason tennis players, or baseball players, or athletes in any fast-moving ball sport don't get into the zone more often. You cannot be in the present if the only information your brain is receiving is about the past, and relative to you as Countermovement, the movement of the ball in any fast-moving ball sport is always the past dimension.

As systems of countermovement in this contact sequence environment we call tennis, we are the *axial temporal element*. That means we exist in time between the past temporal element (the ball) and the future temporal element (contact). We exist *physically* in the present temporal dimension, but how we interface with the other elements of the contact sequence determines in which temporal dimension we exist mentally, emotionally, and spiritually.

Being in the present is a choice. In your normal performance state, you are playing tennis in the past. In your peak performance state, you are playing tennis in the present. If you use your operating system in its normal Serial Mode, you will play tennis in your normal performance state: tennis in the past. But if you choose to use your operating system in its higher-order Parallel Mode, you will be choosing to play tennis in your peak performance state: tennis in the present.

5.4: Serial and Parallel Interface

Stand back for a moment and instead of thinking of yourself as tennis player holding a certain National Tennis Rating Program (NTRP) ranking, see yourself as a human operating system functioning in the contact sequence environment of the tennis court. That's a mouthful, but it's also something that we all have in common as tennis players. We are all, at our fundamental level, highly-organized, Input/Processing/Output (IPO) operating systems, and as IPO operating systems, the efficiency and accuracy of our interface with the action on the tennis court determines the quality of our performance.

This interface between operating system and on-court action begins with visual input, and the quality of that visual input is responsible for the quality of the information being processed by the brain. Using VDF as your visual strategy creates a *Serial Interface* between your operating system and the tennis environment. "Serial" means a stream of sequential bits of information. As you are continuously refocusing on the ball at different locations along its flight line, your eyes are inputting sequential bits of information to your brain about the movement of the ball. Your brain then processes that information sequentially (serial processing), then outputs motor information, also sequentially, to your body (serial output). Thus you create an overall Serial Interface between you, as an operating system, and the action of the tennis court. This Serial Interface begins with the way you use your eyes.

A *Parallel Interface* also begins with how you use your eyes; except in a Parallel Interface you are inputting information to your brain about two things at once: the depth of your contact zone and the location of the ball as it moves toward your contact zone. These two streams of information are sent to your brain simultaneously as parallel streams of information, thus your brain processes both streams of information at the same time (parallel processing), then outputs motor information to your body about the location of the contact point along your pre-defined depth of contact (parallel output). Thus you create an overall Parallel Interface between your operating system and the action on the tennis court.

Of importance is that neither of these methods of interfacing with the tennis environment is right or wrong. A Serial Interface is what it is, an interface between your operating system and the movement of the ball, an interface between you and the past dimension of the contact sequence. Your body is in the present; your mind is in the past. A Serial Interface is a learned system interface, the one you've been learning to use since you were a kid. It's also the system interface of your Normal Performance State.

A Parallel Interface is also a learned interface, but instead of being an interface between your operating system and the movement of the ball, it's an interface between your operating system and the location of the contact point; which is to say, an interface between you, the ball *and* the contact zone. In other words, an interface between you and the past and future dimensions of the contact sequence simultaneously; it is an interface with the present. Your body is in the present and so is your mind. A Parallel Interface is your highest-order system interface, the system interface of your Peak Performance State, the system interface of the zone.

5.5: Letting Go of the Past

When you are first learning how to play tennis in the zone, one of the hardest things to do is to defocus from your opponent and the ball. But when you think about what you are doing temporally when you fix your focus on your contact zone, you will see that you are defocusing from the past (ball) and focusing on the future (contact zone). In essence, you are letting go of the past by connecting to the future. No longer is your focus being controlled by the past elements of the contact sequence, but rather you are taking control of your own focus and placing it where it will do you the most good – on your own immediate future, on your own contact zone.

Of course, this doesn't mean that you can't play good tennis when you focus on the ball. You can. In fact, you can play very good tennis when you focus on the ball, but you won't play your best tennis; you won't enter into your peak performance state because your peak performance state is about being in the present, and as long as you keep focusing on the ball you won't be in the present, you'll be in the past.

This temporal distinction might seem vague and unimportant, but it is a distinction that can help you enter into the higher-order reality of your peak performance state. Focusing on your contact zone switches you from focusing on the past to focusing on the future. You still see the past (your opponent and the ball), but the past no longer controls your focus. Instead, you have taken control of your own focus, and by fixing it on the immediate future of your contact zone, your countermovements will be made according to the future location of the contact point, not the past location of the ball.

The flow of events in every contact sequence is always toward the future, toward the event of contact. The arrow of time always points to the future, and for your operating system to flow smoothly with time; it must first be focused *with* the flow of time, focused on the future.

Which makes more sense to you: for your operating system to be focused *against the flow of time*, focused on the past, or for your operating system to be focused *with the flow of time* – focused on the future?

With Variable-Depth of Focus Input you are focused against the flow of time, but with Fixed-Depth of Focus Input you are focused with the flow of time. It's a no-brainer.

5.6: Flash-Outs

Focusing on my contact zone went completely against everything I had ever learned about how to focus on the tennis court. As kids we were always told to focus on the ball, that's it. That was the height of concentrative excellence. The notion of focusing on the ball was thought to be the purest possible form of visual concentration, and yet every time I went from focusing on the ball to focusing on my contact zone, I went from playing in the norm to playing in the zone. Immediately!

Conversely, whenever I went back to focusing on the ball, I found myself coming out of the zone and returning to my normal performance state. It all seemed backwards, but since FDF kept working for me, I kept practicing it.

And with practice I got more adept at maintaining my fixed- depth of focus. But there were times when I would lose control of my focus momentarily, as if I was taking a snapshot of something that was happening. I called these quick focal snapshots *"flash-outs,"* because that's exactly what they felt like. Instead of staying focused on my contact zone and letting the action take place in my peripheral vision, I would suddenly flash-out on some piece of the action, and with that flash-out I found myself returning to VDF and my normal performance state.

Flash-outs have turned out to be an interesting phenomenon in the process of learning how to play tennis in the zone. Whenever I flashed-out on something, I found that I had trouble with the very next shot, or I mishit the next shot after the flash-out. It was very disconcerting at first. These flash-outs disturbed the flow of my play and caused me to make errors I didn't make when I maintained a fixed-focus on my contact zone.

I found that flash-outs came in several generic flavors. My most common flash-out was on the ball. It happened when I returned to focusing on the ball as my opponent hit it, or as the ball was coming toward my contact zone, or after I made contact and the ball was going away from my contact zone.

At first, flashing-out on the ball was a common focal error. But once I started identifying these flash-outs on the ball, I realized that they were caused by me reverting to the way I had concentrated and focused for so many years. Flashing-out on the ball when my opponent hit it was my old way of seeing where the ball was going, and flashing-out on the ball after I hit it was my old way of getting my success or failure feedback.

What I was finding out through experiencing these same situations in a fixed-focus state was that I could still see whether or not my shots were successful, but by keeping my focus on my contact zone, I also found that I wasn't getting emotionally caught up in the success or failure of my shots. Instead, *I was always focally prepared for the next ball coming toward my contact zone.*

And by focally prepared I mean I was visually and mentally prepared for my opponent's next shot, rather than being visually and mentally caught up in the results of my last shot.

This made sense to me. If my eyes and my mind were focused on my contact zone, then they would be defocused from the results of my last shot. And when my eyes and my mind were defocused from my results, then I would not become emotionally attached to my results.

Emotional detachment via focal detachment!

It was working! I was controlling my emotions by detaching focally from the results of my shots, and all I had to do was keep my focus fixed on my contact zone.

But there was something else happening at the same time. By being visually and mentally focused on my contact zone, I was focally prepared for anything my opponent hit toward my contact zone.

Being emotionally detached while at the same time being totally prepared sounded pretty good to me. In fact, by being mentally and visually focused on my contact zone, I was *anticipating* better than ever before, but in a different way than ever before. My whole upbringing in tennis had taught me to focus on my opponent to anticipate where he was going with his next shot. But the more I worked with fixing my focus on my contact zone, the more I realized that I was anticipating in a completely different way.

5.7: Future Focus and Anticipation

What does it mean to "read your opponent?"

I was taught to focus on my opponent and watch for any physical clues in his strokes that might give away his intentions. Thus I could anticipate where he was going to hit his next shot. For instance, if he rotated his shoulders a certain way or moved his feet a certain way, then I would know beforehand the most likely shot he would hit. This worked, too, sometimes. Other times, it felt like guesswork, and I guessed wrong as often as I guessed right

As I got better a keeping my focus fixed on my contact zone, I found that I was still able to see my opponent's movements in my peripheral vision. It's not like my opponent disappeared or I couldn't see him any more. I could still see everything he was doing; it was just out of focus, peripheral, part of the bigger picture I was seeing.

I also found that my reaction time was much faster when I kept my focus on my contact zone. I was getting to shots that used to get past me. It was as if I knew in advance where they were going, and, in a sense, I did. By prefocusing on my contact zone, I was visually and mentally anticipating not only the future depth of the ball's movement, I was also anticipating the future depth of my countermovement as well as the future depth of the contact event.

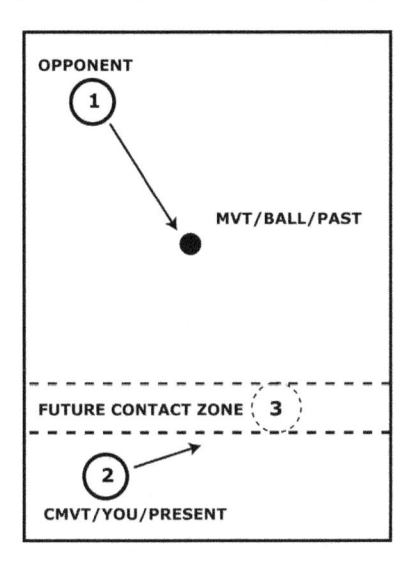

```
            OPPONENT
               (1)
                 \
                  \
                   ↘
                     ●  MVT/BALL/PAST

    - - - - - - - - - - - - - - -
    FUTURE CONTACT ZONE ( 3 )
    - - - - - - - - - - - - - - -
                    ↗
               (2)
           CMVT/YOU/PRESENT
```

The contact zone represents three futures in one.

- The future depth of movement.
- The future depth of countermovement.
- The future depth of contact.

Webster's Dictionary defines anticipation as:

1. A prior action that takes into account a later (future) action.
2. The act of looking forward.
3. Visualization of a future event or state.

Prefocusing on my contact zone seemed to fit the definition in every way. Prefocusing on my contact zone is a prior action (prefocusing) that takes into account a later action (contact). Prefocusing on my contact zone is an act of looking forward to the future depth of movement, countermovement and contact. And finally, prefocusing on my contact zone literally visualizes the future depth of the most important event in the game – the contact event.

I was beginning to see anticipation in a completely different context. Instead of focusing on my opponent to read his strokes (a prior action) and thus anticipate a future action (where he was going to hit the ball), *I was prefocusing on the future depth of any of his shots.*

5.8: Two Visual Pathways of the Brain

But this different approach to anticipation was only a part of the reason I was getting to more shots than before and feeling that my reactions were faster. My reactions actually were faster, and according to Dr. Michael Mesches, a Denver neuroscientist, this is why:

> *"Visual information from the tennis environment enters your brain through two visual pathways. One is called the "What Pathway" and the other is called the "Where Pathway." The What Pathway is relatively slow in terms of neural pathways. It takes approximately 200 to 300 milliseconds to consciously evolve an awareness of what you are looking at and then respond to it."*

In other words, when you focus on your opponent, it can take up to a third of a second to "consciously evolve an awareness" or to "read" what your opponent is doing.

Have you ever been in a ready position at the net when your doubles partner serves a lousy second serve that bounces halfway in the service court and you watch transfixed as your opponent crushes a huge forehand that screams past you for a winner in your alley?

You would have made a move on it, but by the time you saw it, the ball was already past you. This happens to everyone who plays the game, and it's a good example of your What Pathway at work in the tennis environment.

It took your brain approximately 300 milliseconds to evolve a conscious awareness of what just happened when your opponent crushed his huge forehand, and then you had to respond to it. But in the 300 milliseconds it took your brain to register what just happened, the return was already past you. In the time it took you to "read" your opponent's shot, the ball was already past you. Your slow reaction to the shot was a function of being focused in the wrong place at the wrong time and using your slowest visual pathway – the What Pathway.

You blame it on your partner's lousy second serve; your partner blames it on your lousy reflexes, and you're both right. Unfortunately, you can't do much about your partner's lousy second serve. That's his problem. But you can do something about your lousy reflexes.

Dr. Mesches continues:

> "While the What Pathway is relatively slow in evolving a response to the action on the tennis court, the Where Pathway, by comparison, is extremely fast. Response time using your Where Pathway is approximately 50 milliseconds as compared to 300 milliseconds using your What Pathway. Locating the contact point on a predefined focal plane is a prime example of using your Where-Pathway in tennis."

Do the math. 50 milliseconds using the Where Pathway versus 300 milliseconds using the What Pathway. That means response time using your Where Pathway is up to six times faster than response time using your What Pathway.

SIX TIMES FASTER! No wonder my reflexes felt so much faster when I was in the zone. They actually were!

According to Dr. Mesches:

"There is no contest as to which pathway leads to a quicker response to the movement of the ball. When you are watching the ball (VDF visual input pattern), you are trying to keep the image of the ball on your fovea, which causes you to use the What Pathway. This pathway is designed to detect details; it is not designed to detect motion. It is also the slower of the two visual pathways at determining the ball's speed and direction.

When you are locating the contact point on a fixed focal plane (FDF visual input pattern), you are using the Where Pathway, which is specifically designed to detect motion, but it does not detect fine details. It is also the faster of the two visual pathways at determining the ball's speed and direction and how to react to it. Of importance is that both pathways are always active.

The What Pathway is the predominant visual pathway we use for the vast majority of our daily activities. It is also the pathway we are taught to use when we begin playing tennis, because we are taught to "watch the ball" with our fovea.

The Where Pathway is designed to detect moving objects and to send that information to the area of our brain that is designed to respond to that information, and to do so very quickly! What that means to you as a tennis player is that your response time will be much faster if you use your Where Pathway when you play tennis, but in order to use your Where Pathway, you have to stop focusing on the ball (VDF visual input pattern) and start focusing on your contact zone (FDF visual input pattern).

Importantly, the Where Pathway has direct connections to the premotor cortex, the region of the brain that feeds directly into the motor cortex, which controls your voluntary movements." (personal communication, August, 2000)

The bottom line is that you have choices as to how you use your visual and mental focus on the tennis court. You can let the ball or your opponent control your focus, in which case you will be using your What Pathway to respond to the action in front of you. Or you can take control of your own focus and lock it squarely on your contact zone, in which case you will be using your Where Pathway to respond up to six times faster to the action in front of you.

As for anticipation, these focal choices have huge ramifications. You can anticipate your opponent's next shot by watching his/her strokes, in which case you are again using your What Pathway, and by the time you read what your opponent is doing, it's already been done; it's already in the past. That means, very simply, that you are trying to anticipate the future by focusing on the past.

Or, you can choose another way. By focusing on your contact zone, you are simultaneously focusing on the future depth of movement, the future depth of countermovement and the future depth of contact. You are effectively anticipating the future by focusing on the future of all three elements of the tennis environment.

Which method of anticipation makes more sense to you:

1. Anticipating the future by focusing on the past?
2. Anticipating the future by focusing on three futures in one?

You get to pick, but I'll take Door #2 every time.

5.9: Heightened Visual Awareness

The Fifth Step makes several assumptions:

— First, it assumes that you have gone through the other steps

and that you are able to fix your focus on your contact zone and locate the 3-Point with your eyes.
- Second, it assumes that you have spent time practicing Fixed-Depth of Focus Input from the different depths of the court – backcourt, midcourt and forecourt.
- Finally, it assumes that you can distinguish between your normal performance state and your peak performance state both in terms of your higher level of play and your higher-order conscious state.

Remember, playing tennis in the zone will never feel the same as playing tennis in the norm. Your peak performance state is a combination of a more efficient and more accurate operating mode – a Parallel Mode (that's what makes you play better), and a higher-order conscious state – a flow state (that's what makes you feel different).

The more you experience playing tennis in the zone, the more familiar you will become with both your higher level of performance and your higher-order conscious state. Breaking the zone down into its component parts will help you understand the experience intellectually, but nothing can replace the actual experience of being in the zone.

In fact, the only way you can learn how to play tennis in the zone is by doing it. You can read about it until you're cross-eyed. You can know everything there is to know about human systems dynamics, the Visual/Cognitive/Motor interface, the behavioral psychology of flow, but until you experience the zone for yourself, until you actually make the switch from playing in the norm to playing in the zone, you're just talking the talk. To truly understand the zone, you must walk the walk. You have to do it.

The Fifth Step is walking the walk. You must be in the zone to experience this step because it is all about identifying the flash-outs that take you *out* of the zone, and you can't come out of the zone unless you are *in* the zone in the first place.

The Fifth Step will also give you direct experience with the flow component of heightened visual awareness. Players who have experienced the zone in tennis report:

- Seeing the ball better than normal.
- That the ball seems bigger than normal.
- That the ball seems to be moving in slow motion.

This heightened state of visual awareness happens for a reason. When players slip into the zone, they also slip into a Fixed-Depth of Focus input pattern, and it is this FDF input pattern that is responsible for their heightened state of visual awareness. In other words, you don't see the ball better because you are in the zone; you see the ball better because when you are in the zone, you are using FDF as your visual input pattern, and with your focus fixed on your contact zone, every ball coming toward your contact zone will also be coming into focus. Quite naturally, this will seem like you are seeing the ball better than normal. And why wouldn't it? The ball is always coming into focus as it comes toward your contact zone. You can't help but see it better!

The confusion comes the next day when you remember how much better you "saw" the ball when you were in the zone. Here's how that heightened state of visual awareness usually gets translated:

"I was seeing the ball better than normal yesterday when I was in the zone, so obviously I must have been watching the ball better than normal yesterday when I was in the zone. I must have been totally focused on the ball. So, that's what I'm going to do again today. I'm going to totally focus on the ball and then I'll see it better, just like when I was in the zone."

Only when you were in the zone, you saw the ball better for exactly the opposite reason! You saw it better because you were *not* focused on it. You were focused instead on your contact zone and the ball was coming *into* focus.

But today, when you try even harder to keep the ball in focus, what you are really doing is locking yourself into a Variable-Depth of Focus input pattern (serial input), which, in turn, will lock you into a Serial Operating Mode. So, instead of playing tennis in the zone and seeing the ball better, you will be playing tennis in the norm and wondering why the heck the ball is moving so damn fast and always out of focus. Seeing the ball better is one of the most difficult of the zone characteristics to understand, and yet it is a common occurrence when you are in your Parallel Mode. As you become more familiar with your Parallel Mode, you will also become more familiar with maintaining your focus on your contact zone and seeing what the game looks like when you engage your Where Pathway.

You will still have to fight:

- The urge to focus on the ball as it moves back and forth across the net (flash-outs on the ball).
- The urge to focus on your opponent to see what he/she is going to do next (a flash-out on your opponent).
- The urge to focus on the open court to see where you are going to hit your next shot (a flash-out on placement).

Removing these flash-outs from your game is what the Fifth Step is all about. Here's how it works:

- Play out a rally while visually locating the different 3-Points along the surface of your imaginary window.
- If you are successful at visually locating the 3-Point, say "yes." If you do not locate the 3-Point say "no."
- If you did not locate the 3-Point, then you flashed-out on something.

— Identify your flash-out.

Remember, if you are able to locate the 3-Point on your imaginary window, you will also be able to make contact at the 3-Point. So, don't worry about how you make contact at the 3-Point or where your shot is going after you make contact at the 3-Point. That's not the objective of this step. The objective is to visually locate every 3-Point that comes into your contact zone during the course of each point.

You can even keep score on your visual progress. If you located four out of five 3-Points that came into your contact zone, then you scored 80% on that particular point. If you didn't locate any, then you scored zero, and you were obviously focused on something other than your contact zone or you flashed-out on something during the course of the point.

Flash-outs will happen. Expect them to happen. Nobody scores 100% on this visual task when they first give it a try. Besides, that's not the objective. The objective is to identify what is causing you to lose your focus. What are you flashing-out on?

- Are you flashing-out on the ball, either before contact or after contact?
- Are you flashing-out on your opponent to see what he is going to do with his shot?
- Are you flashing-out on the open court to see where you are going to hit your shot?
- Maybe you are flashing-out on your footwork or your looping backswing or how much topspin you are going to put on your shot.
- Maybe you are flashing-out on who is playing on the court next to you.
- Maybe you are flashing-out on what's for dinner.

Flash-outs come in many forms and flavors and your objective in this visual exercise is to identify them when they happen. But also to recognize when they don't happen, and there will be an ever-increasing number of points in which you have no flash-outs at all. Recognize these times, too, because when you have successfully located every 3-Point that comes into your contact zone during the course of the point, then you have successfully maintained a Fixed-Depth of Focus throughout that point.

That means you have maintained your Parallel Mode for the whole point. You have maintained the zone for one complete point. Now all you have to do is maintain it for the next point and build your ability to maintain the zone throughout each point of each game of each set of each match of each tournament that you play.

Sounds like a daunting task, doesn't it? Perhaps it sounds impossible. But for players who play the game of tennis expressly for the purpose of getting into the zone, there is no other challenge of regard. Winning and losing carry the same weight – none. Playing tennis in the zone is not about winning and losing. It's about maintaining the zone while you play. Therein lies the greatest challenge in the game. Therein you will find the truest meaning of the game.

THE FIFTH STEP

Objective: to identify any loss of focus from your contact zone. To identify flash-outs.

- Begin by simply playing out a rally point (NO SERVE). Your visual objective is to locate every 3-Point that enters into your contact zone.
- Immediate verbal feedback: "yes" if you locate the 3-Point, "no" if you don't.
- If the answer is no, then you flashed-out on something, and your objective is to identify your flash-out.

Common flash-outs:

- Flash-out on the ball (before you make contact or after you make contact)
- Flash-out on your opponent (to read what he/she is going to do)
- Flash-out on placement (the target).
- Flash-out on technique (how you do your strokes).

That's it. That's all there is to the Fifth Step. Identify your flash-outs as you play out rally points. You'll be surprised at how long you can maintain your focus once you learn what causes you to lose it.

FLASH-OUT TABLE

	Opponent	Ball	Bounce	Placement	Technique	Outcome	Other
Backcourt Rally							
Midcourt Approach							
Forecourt Volley							
Transition BC to FC							
Serve Return							
Other							

This flash-out table can be used to help identify your flash-outs. Before you can play out points in a Fixed-Focus State, you must first be able to identify the people, places, and things that are causing you to lose your focus. Using this table can help you identify these distractions, and once you become aware of your flash-outs, you can remove these visual and mental distractions from your game.

Self-Rating Your Progress

Once again, the tasks you are measuring on the Feedback page are:

1. Visualizing an imaginary window in front of you at a comfortable arm's length. (Visualize window)
2. Using your eyes to locate the contact point on your imaginary window. (Locate the 3-Point)
3. Immediate verbal "yes/no" feedback percentage (FB%)
4. Identify your flash-outs

Your rating system for visualizing and locating the 3-Point on your window in each of the drills is the same 1-2-3-4 rating scale.

1. Never
2. Some of the time
3. Most of the time
4. Always

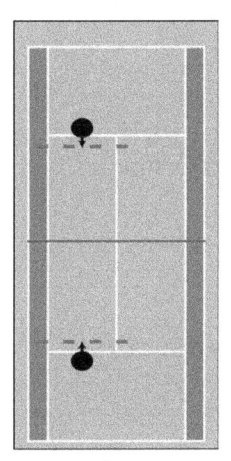

Drill 1

Circle where you would rate yourself in each category.

How successfully did you:		
Visualize Window	**Locate 3**	**FB%**
1 2 3 4	1 2 3 4	1 2 3 4

Flashouts

Opponent/Ball/Bounce/Placement/Technique/Outcome

Drill 2

Circle where you would rate yourself in each category.

How successfully did you:		
Visualize Window	**Locate 3**	**FB%**
1 2 3 4	1 2 3 4	1 2 3 4

Flashouts

Opponent/Ball/Bounce/Placement/Technique/Outcome

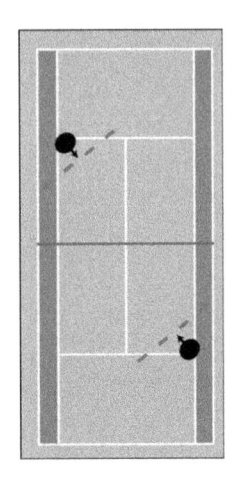

Drill 3

Circle where you would rate yourself in each category.

How successfully did you:		
Visualize Window	**Locate 3**	**FB%**
1 2 3 4	1 2 3 4	1 2 3 4

Flashouts

Opponent/Ball/Bounce/Placement/Technique/Outcome

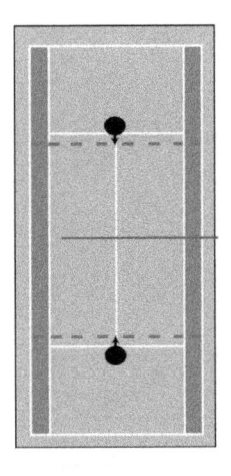

Drill 4

Circle where you would rate yourself in each category.

How successfully did you:		
Visualize Window	**Locate 3**	**FB%**
1 2 3 4	1 2 3 4	1 2 3 4

Flashouts

Opponent/Ball/Bounce/Placement/Technique/Outcome

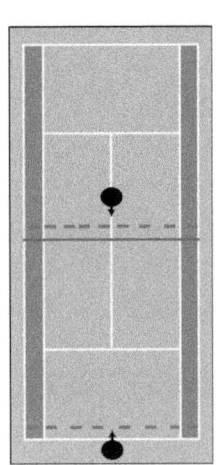

Drill 5

Circle where you would rate yourself in each category.

How successfully did you:		
Visualize Window	**Locate 3**	**FB%**
1 2 3 4	1 2 3 4	1 2 3 4

Flashouts

Opponent/Ball/Bounce/Placement/Technique/Outcome

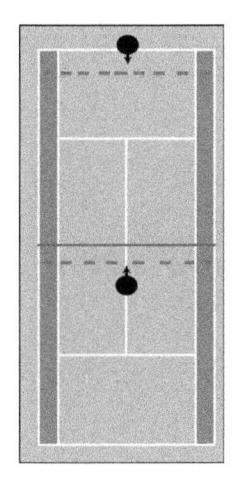

Drill 6

Circle where you would rate yourself in each category.

How successfully did you:		
Visualize Window	**Locate 3**	**FB%**
1 2 3 4	1 2 3 4	1 2 3 4

Flashouts

Opponent/Ball/Bounce/Placement/Technique/Outcome

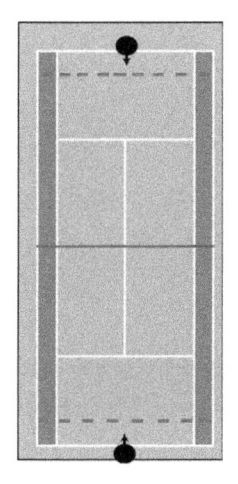

Drill 7

Circle where you would rate yourself in each category.

How successfully did you:		
Visualize Window	**Locate 3**	**FB%**
1 2 3 4	1 2 3 4	1 2 3 4

Flashouts

Opponent/Ball/Bounce/Placement/Technique/Outcome

In these drills you are learning how to control your visual and mental focus as you move through the different depths of the court. If you are not experiencing the zone, then you are probably trying to hit the ball over the net (create an outcome) rather than locate the contact point on your imaginary window and stay in the process.

Remember, the zone is about the process not the outcome.

Enjoy the zone.

Chapter 6: Change

"The greatest power that a person possesses is the power to choose."
— J. Martin Kohe

Key Subjects
6.1: The Zone and Sport Psychology
6.2: Being in the Present
6.3: Hitting the 3-Point
6.4: Operation

6.1: The Zone and Sport Psychology

I always tell people that playing tennis in the zone is not really about tennis. It's about being in the present when you play tennis. It's about the temporal dimension you create on the tennis court when you interface with the past and the future simultaneously. This past/future interface, or Parallel Interface, creates the temporal dimension of the present, and it is when you are "in the present" that you experience the synthesis of the higher-order physical, emotional, mental and spiritual components of flow.

Synthesizing these different components into a single, unified behavioral state is the main goal of sport psychology. According to Dr. Othon Kesend, a sport psychologist from Boulder, Colorado:

> *"The Holy Grail of sport performance is playing in the zone, an elusive state of performance in which athletes effortlessly play at their highest level of performance. The main purpose of sport psychology is to help athletes achieve this state, but no sports psychologist can teach you how to do this 'at will' no matter what their claims.*
>
> *We sport psychologists are often addressing multiple behavioral concerns and work toward correcting and balancing these elements in order to support an improved and more consistent level of performance. But it will not guarantee performance in the zone. Sometimes the various elements we address as sport psychologists will integrate in such a way that the athlete enters the zone, but this is not reproducible by choice."*

There's the rub. Sport psychologists believes the zone is not reproducible by choice, and because of this, we, as athletes, have come to believe there is nothing we can do to make the zone happen. We can prepare for it. We can go through the neuro-physical relaxation and visualization techniques available to us. We can breathe properly, eat properly and train properly. We can study various religions and spiritual belief systems. We can meditate, we can concentrate, but according to the sport psychology community, we cannot make it happen. We can only set the stage for the zone.

The Parallel Mode Process suggests something completely different. It suggests that by switching from your Serial Mode to your Parallel Mode, you very definitely *can* make the zone happen by choice.

Dr. Kesend continues:

> *"The Parallel Mode Process works in a singular and simple way with the human operating system. By using the Fixed-Depth of Focus method of input that engages the visual/cognitive system*

in a parallel processing state, both hemispheres of the brain are engaged equally compared to the hemispheric dominance of our normal Serial Mode state. In this whole-brain state we experience a significant increase in brain power, which integrates and optimizes all levels of functioning and performance – physical, mental, emotional and spiritual. In this state you are playing in the present so thoughts and feelings created in the past don't intrude. All of you is truly in the game.

Typically, sport psychologists teach staying in the task at hand. But the task at hand is always changing, so, in effect, the athlete is using a variable focus, a focus which is always changing, making moment-to-moment responsiveness difficult and, in some cases, impossible.

It's much easier to maintain one constant focus, which is what you do in your Parallel Mode. In the whole-brain state that your Parallel Mode produces, everything unfolds as a continuum within and as part of the constant focus. It's like a movie screen, which is constant but contains the continually changing events.

A constant singular focus allows for our minds and bodies to quiet, and in this state experience a higher level of perception; an ability to see much more of what is going on, yet to much more rapidly process it and respond effortlessly, quickly, efficiently and effectively to each moment of the game." (personal communication, October, 2002)

There has been a great deal of research and development in the area of sport psychology since the 1970's. One of the giants in sport psychology who turned his talents to the tennis industry is Dr. Jim Loehr. His body of work over the last four decades has produced a wider understanding of the importance of mental toughness in competition, on the court and off - in sports, in business, and in life.

Along with Timothy Gallwey, Dr. Mihali Csikszentmihalyi and a handful of other visionary coaches and teachers, Dr. Loehr saw that the key to this peak experience we call the zone lay not in how well you controlled the game, but in how well you controlled the physical, emotional, mental, and spiritual aspects of the self. I owe much of my understanding of the psychological side of the performance coin to these teachers who dared to investigate this uncharted territory long before it became fashionable.

Unlike traditional sport psychology, however, which directly addresses the mental side of the performance coin, the Parallel Mode Process directly addresses the operational side of the same coin. The side of the coin you can't see but is always present.

There would be no performance behaviors at all if your operating system weren't interfacing in the background. In other words, you can't have behavior without operation, nor can you have operation without behavior.

6.2: Being in the Present

Our normal temporal interface in tennis and in life is a temporal interface with the past; the immediate past granted, but the past nonetheless. In tennis, this temporal interface with the immediate past is created by focusing on the ball, the past element of the contact sequence environment. We can also create a temporal interface with the immediate future by simply focusing on the contact zone, which is where the future element of the contact sequence environment – contact – will be located.

The difference in these two temporal interfaces is the difference between playing tennis in the norm and playing tennis in the zone. One temporal interface, our default, past interface actually goes against the flow of time, while our higher-order future interface goes with the flow of time. All that is required to change from playing against the flow of time to playing with the flow of time is a change in the focus of your eyes.

Yet as simple as this temporal change might sound, it is perhaps the most confusing behavioral change we face in the game. So much of our game is based on focusing on the past elements of the tennis environment - the people, places and objects to which we give over control of our focus. But because we function quite well in this past temporal interface, we find it very difficult to change. We are unwilling to change something that works and feels normal for something that feels so different, even if it works much better.

Change is not something humans like. We like stability. We like security. When something works, we stick with it and try like crazy to make it work better. Asking someone to suddenly change something that works, something to which he/she has grown accustomed, is asking for more than some people are willing to give. To change from playing tennis in the norm to playing tennis in the zone you must do a complete turnabout in your temporal interface. You must change from focusing on the near past to focusing on the near future. That's a temporal 180, and it requires not only a change in your focal behavior, but also a change in your physical, emotional, mental, and spiritual behaviors.

Operationally, you are reversing your operating system's temporal interface with the game. You are changing from a past temporal interface (serial) to a future temporal interface (parallel). The difference is that when you are in a past temporal interface, focused on the ball, you can't see the future; you can't see your contact zone. But when you are in a future temporal interface, focused on your contact zone, you can still "see" your opponent, the ball, and the court. In other words, when you are focused on your future you can still see your past. More importantly, when you are seeing the past and the future simultaneously, you are creating the most elusive temporal interface of all: the unified temporal interface of the present.

This unified temporal interface - being in the present - lies at the core of your peak performance state. Being in the present is causal to the higher-order physical, emotional, mental and spiritual behaviors you experience when you are in the zone. Higher order behaviors such as:

- A loss of self-consciousness;
- Total absorption in the task at hand;
- Total concentration;
- Immediate and unambiguous feedback;
- Action/awareness merging (automatic pilot);
- Time transformation;
- A sense of control.

You experience an awareness of the game that you cannot experience when you are in a past temporal interface because your normal interface is limited to that which exists in your immediate past.

There is nothing wrong with a past temporal interface, mind you. In fact, it works very well for us. But it is not our most all-inclusive interface because of its inherent temporal limitations (past only). In order to break out of the bondage of these temporal limitations it is necessary to completely change your temporal interface, and to do that, you have to stop focusing on the immediate past (ball) and start focusing on the immediate future (contact zone).

6.3: Hitting the 3-Point

The more familiar I became with playing tennis in the zone, the more familiar I became with the actual event of contact. I knew that every contact event contained three elements:

- The ball,
- My racquet
- A contact point.

This made me think that there was more than one way to go about creating a contact event. I could use my racquet to hit the ball, in which case the contact event would contain the ball, my racquet and a contact point located somewhere in my contact zone.

Or, I could use my racquet to hit the 3-Point, in which case I would still have the same three elements of contact: the ball, my racquet and a contact point located somewhere in the contact zone. Only this time the contact point wouldn't be located just *somewhere* in my contact zone, it would be located at the exact point the ball first entered the space and time of my contact zone. When I hit the 3-Point, contact would be located at the Primary Contact Point.

When I first tried "hitting the 3-Point," I didn't try to do anything with the 3-Point except hit it with my racquet. I knew that if I hit the 3-Point, I would also be creating a contact event with the ball, but instead of concentrating on hitting the ball at the 3-Point, I would concentrate on hitting the 3-Point itself. I wanted to observe what happened without judging the results.

Theoretically, I knew that if all I did was hit the 3-Point when and where it appeared at my contact zone, then I would be creating a contact event at the exact moment the ball first entered my contact zone. Contact at the Primary Contact Point meant that my contact would be positively timed - every time.

I was curious about what would happen, and what made this interesting to me was that I was not trying to hit the ball over the net. I was only trying to hit the 3-Point with whatever stroke my operating system came up with.

This required me to keep my focus firmly fixed on my contact zone and locate every 3-Point with my eyes. Fortunately, I was getting more proficient at Fixed-Depth of Focus Input, so I was able to continuously locate the 3-Point, which allowed me to see what would happen if all I did was hit as many 3-Points in a row as possible. Technique didn't matter, form didn't matter, and results didn't matter. All that mattered was successfully completing my objective of hitting as many 3-Points in a row as possible.

For some reason this all made sense to me. The concept seemed logical. Contacting the 3-Point meant that I would also be contacting the ball, but it also meant that I would be creating a contact event at the Primary Contact Point. That combination should be enough to cause the ball to go back over the net and into the court. What the heck. It was an experiment. I had nothing to lose, and, as an objective, hitting the 3-Point took away the pressure of getting the ball back over the net. I wasn't trying to hit a good shot. I was only trying to hit the 3-Point. Nothing more; nothing less.

What I observed amazed me, surprised me, fascinated me, and made me want more of the same. I found that almost every time I contacted the 3-Point with my racquet, the ball went back over the net and into the court. I wasn't trying for these results, mind you, they were just happening, and I realized they were happening for very logical spatial and temporal reasons, foremost of which was the fact that my strokes, whatever they looked like as I hit the 3-Point, were all positively timed. The contact event was occurring at or very near the Primary Contact Point every time, and the result was almost always positive movement of the ball back over the net and into the court. I seldom missed a shot.

As a result, hitting the 3-Point became my performance objective instead of hitting the ball. When I played to hit as many 3-Points as possible, my whole game transcended its normal performance boundaries.

But it was not just the higher level of performance that got my attention. It was the higher-order consciousness, the total concentration, the total focus and flow that grabbed my attention.

The more familiar I became with hitting the 3-Point instead of the ball, the more I realized that each of the behavioral components of this elusive flow state were actually occurring simultaneously. When I would finish a game, a set, or a match, I would look back at the match and realize that I had been playing on automatic pilot. I would look back and realize that I had played the whole match without worrying about how I appeared out there on the court, without worrying about winning or losing, or whether I was performing as well as I could. There was no self involved, no ego. All I had been doing was playing a selfless game of hitting the 3-Point.

I was "aware" of the positive results I was getting, but only peripherally aware. I wasn't focused on the outcome of my shots, and since I didn't get focally attached to the outcome, I also didn't get mentally or emotionally attached. Instead, I simply maintained a fixed-focus on my contact zone and continued hitting the next 3-Point. The results took care of themselves without any focal attention from me. I was finding out experientially what it meant to totally let go of the outcome.

The more I experimented with the objective of hitting the 3-Point, the more I learned about the behavioral components of flow, and the more I realized that my experimental attitude played a big role in the process. By playing the game to learn and to experiment, I found myself relieved of the burden of winning. In fact, I found that playing to learn was much more productive than playing to win. Whenever I played to win, I found myself getting caught up in whether I was winning or losing the match. If I was winning, then my self-image was pretty darn good, but if I started missing shots or losing, then my self-confidence and my self-image went straight down the tubes with Mr. Ego.

As I continued with this performance goal of hitting the 3-Point and playing to learn, I no longer got emotionally attached to winning or losing. I couldn't get emotionally attached because I was never focally attached to the outcome of my shots. Instead, I was completely absorbed in the process of hitting the next 3-Point with my racquet; learning how to do that; trying to do that and nothing else.

This task of hitting the 3-Point evolved to stroking the 3-Point, top-spinning the 3-Point, slicing the 3-Point, lobbing the 3-Point, directing the 3-Point. In other words, I could cause the ball to go wherever I wanted it to go or do whatever I wanted it to do without trying to make it go anywhere or do anything. As strange as that sounds, by simply doing something different with every 3-Point, I found that the ball responded very nicely to the various contact events I created each time I did something different to the 3-Point.

This goal of hitting the 3-Point evolved to an overall performance objective that seemed to tie together everything that I had been doing up to that point; a natural progression in the evolution of my own learning. Getting into the zone was no longer the challenge. That part was getting easier every day. But as I got better at hitting the 3-Point, I found that I was also able to maintain the zone for longer periods of time, and I was doing it by maintaining my Parallel Mode of operation.

By simply maintaining a Parallel Mode with its unique Parallel Interface, I was also maintaining the higher-order state of flow. The process of getting into and maintaining the zone was becoming more natural for me the more I practiced switching to a Parallel Mode. The elusive and unusual flow state with all its synthesized flow behaviors was neither elusive nor unusual any more. It was becoming my preferred state, both on and off the court. Being in the present was not only improving my on-court game, it was improving my off-court game as well.

Being in the present means being present for whatever is going on in your life, and being present does wonders for things like relationships and productivity at work, not to mention what life can be like when you are free from the ponderous bondage of self. I was finding out that not only could I play the game unselfconsciously, but I could also translate that same process into living life unselfconsciously. What a difference that has made in my life! Living in the present is fun! Living in the present is exciting! Living in the present is challenging; a perpetual learning experience. Life is new again, every day.

I used to hate getting up in the morning, dreading the boredom of another day of teaching out-of-shape, overweight, people how to turn their shoulders and move their feet. But once I started teaching people how to play tennis in the zone, everything changed. The boredom disappeared. I was no longer trying to teach sound biomechanical techniques to someone whose real problem was that a tennis ball moving 30 to 40 mph was the fastest moving object they had ever related to in their life. Being overweight and out-of-shape was not the problem. The problem was visual. Most people are capable of hitting the ball over the net and into the court even if they are overweight and out-of-shape. The reason they aren't very successful is that their eyes are giving their brains lousy visual information about the location of the contact point. Add 20 extra pounds and a pack-and-a-half of Marlboros to the equation and you've got a tennis teacher's nightmare.

But when you take away the lousy visual input, replace it with Fixed-Depth of Focus Input and a Parallel Mode of operation, what you get is an overweight, out-of-shape player relating to the same fast-moving object in their peak performance state. Suddenly, the ball starts going back and forth over the net more often and the game immediately becomes fun. When players are having fun, they keep coming back. Pretty soon the extra 20 pounds have disappeared, the smokes are trashed and you're looking at a very different person.

Not everyone is willing to change, but change happens. It happened to me. And if I can change, anybody can.

6.4: Operation

In tennis, human beings are all the same in one very fundamental way. We are all operating systems trying to interface with the elements of the tennis environment. While that might sound dehumanizing, it is perhaps one of our most human characteristics. We all have the same fundamental operating system, and that operating system is capable of interfacing with the tennis environment in more than one way. Interface in your Serial Mode and you get your normal performance state with its normal level of play and its normal behavioral state. With a Serial Interface you get tennis in the norm.

Interface with the same tennis environment in your Parallel Mode and you get your peak performance state with its higher level of play and its higher-order behavioral state. With a Parallel Interface you get tennis in the zone. *Remember, you don't play better tennis because you are in the zone; you play better tennis because when you are in the zone, you are functioning in your most efficient and accurate operating mode – your Parallel Mode.*

When you are in your Parallel Mode:

- Your input is more accurate due to Fixed Depth of Focus;
- Your response time is faster due to the Where Pathway;
- Your timing is better due to contact at the 3-Point;
- Your anticipation is better due to Future Focus.

All of these characteristics of physical performance are heightened, so quite naturally, your level of play is heightened. In short, you can't help but play better when you switch to your Parallel Mode. You also don't experience a flow state because you are in the zone. You experience this flow state because a Parallel Interface creates the temporal and spatial dimension of the present, and when you are in the present, the behavioral components of flow are automatically synthesized into a unified flow state.

So both the higher-level of performance and the higher-order behavioral state are caused by switching to your Parallel Mode with its unique Parallel Interface with the tennis environment. When I teach people how to play tennis in the zone, I teach them how to switch to their Parallel Mode and thus create this Parallel Interface on the tennis court. In short, I teach people how to play tennis in the zone by teaching them how to be in the present when they play tennis.

What has always amazed me about this process we call playing tennis in the zone is that, contrary to conventional wisdom, the zone absolutely can be made to happen. Furthermore, it can be made to happen immediately. You just change from playing in your Serial Mode to playing in your Parallel Mode, and immediately you're playing in the zone.

That's when something very special and very human happens. You get a chance to experience yourself in your highest-order performance state just as if you had gone through the process of synthesizing the behavioral components of flow. All you have to do is switch from your Serial Mode to your Parallel Mode; the behavioral synthesis happens automatically.

Sound too easy?

Think about it. In those times when you slipped into the zone for no apparent reason, something very subtle must have happened; something so subtle that you didn't notice it when it happened. It's as if this relaxed, concentrative state suddenly swept over you and you immediately started playing the game better than ever before. You sensed the change come over you, and as you started to play at a higher level, you knew deep down inside that this was the way you could really play the game. You knew this was the real you, the true you, the whole you playing the game. But it all seemed to happen for no apparent reason.

Guess what? There was and is a reason. What happened just prior to the zone coming over you was a subtle change in your visual and mental focus. A change from a Variable-Depth of Focus to a Fixed-Depth of Focus.

Subtle? What is subtler than a change in the focus of your eyes?

Immediate? The change from VDF to FDF causes an immediate change from a Serial Interface (playing tennis in the past) to a Parallel Interface (playing tennis in the present).

No apparent reason? The reason is certainly not very apparent, but there is a reason. The reason is right in front of your eyes. In fact, it *is* your eyes. More exactly, it is your visual focus. Your visual focus is both subtle and immediate, and it is causal to the creation of a Parallel Interface on the court.

Create a Parallel Interface and you go immediately into the zone. No waiting in line, no hassles, and best of all, it doesn't cost you a dime. It does, however, come with a price tag.

The cost of the playing in the zone is your ego.

THE SIXTH STEP

Once again, start in a controlled situation with both you and your partner at midcourt. This time, your feedback is not on your visual input pattern (locating the 3-Point), but rather on making the distinction between hitting the ball and hitting the contact point itself – the 3-Point. Your feedback is "Yes" if you hit the 3-Point and "No" if you hit the ball.

As you become more familiar with contacting the 3-Point, start to extend the depth of field between you and your practice partner, continuing Yes/No feedback on the distinction between hitting the ball and hitting the 3-Point.

When you can make this distinction on a wide variety of shots from different positions on the court, you will begin to see a difference in the level of your performance created by consistent, positive timing. Remember, when you hit the 3-Point you will also be hitting the ball. But when you hit the ball, you might not be hitting it at the 3-Point.

Self-Rating Your Progress

Here are the tasks you are measuring on the Feedback page:

1. Visualizing an imaginary window in front of you at a comfortable arm's length. (Visualize window)
2. Using your racquet to "hit" the contact point on your imaginary window. (Hit the 3-Point)
3. Immediate verbal "yes/no" feedback percentage. (FB%)
4. Don't forget to identify your flash-outs!

Your rating system for visualizing and locating the 3-Point on your window in each of the drills is the same 1-2-3-4 rating scale.

1. Never
2. Some of the time
3. Most of the time
4. Always

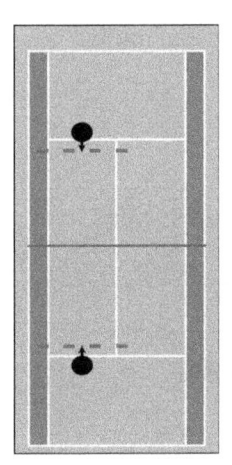

Drill 1

Circle where you would rate yourself in each category.

How successfully did you:		
Visualize Window	**Hit the 3-Point**	**FB%**
1 2 3 4	1 2 3 4	1 2 3 4

Flashouts

Opponent/Ball/Bounce/Placement/Technique/Outcome

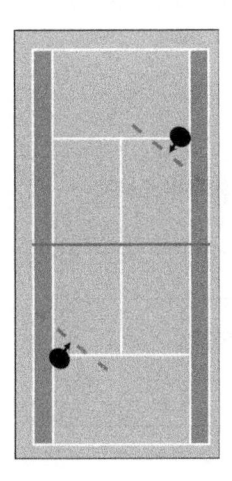

Drill 2

Circle where you would rate yourself in each category.

How successfully did you:		
Visualize Window	**Hit the 3-Point**	**FB%**
1 2 3 4	1 2 3 4	1 2 3 4

Flashouts

Opponent/Ball/Bounce/Placement/Technique/Outcome

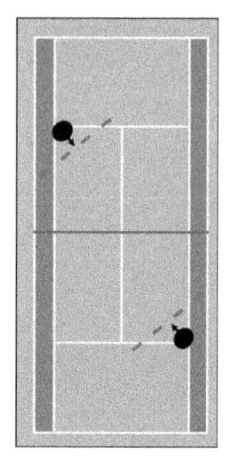

Drill 3

Circle where you would rate yourself in each category.

How successfully did you:		
Visualize Window	Hit the 3-Point	FB%
1 2 3 4	1 2 3 4	1 2 3 4

Flashouts

Opponent/Ball/Bounce/Placement/Technique/Outcome

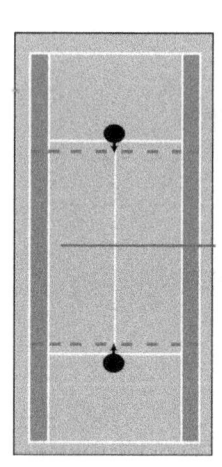

Drill 4

Circle where you would rate yourself in each category.

How successfully did you:		
Visualize Window	Hit the 3-Point	FB%
1 2 3 4	1 2 3 4	1 2 3 4

Flashouts

Opponent/Ball/Bounce/Placement/Technique/Outcome

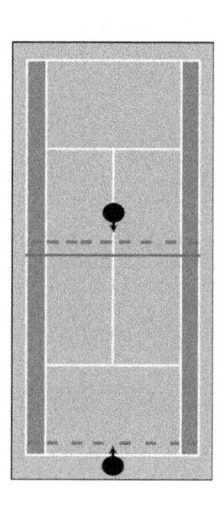

Drill 5

Circle where you would rate yourself in each category.

How successfully did you:		
Visualize Window	Hit the 3-Point	FB%
1 2 3 4	1 2 3 4	1 2 3 4

Flashouts

Opponent/Ball/Bounce/Placement/Technique/Outcome

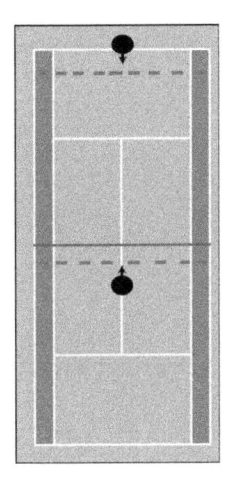

Drill 6

Circle where you would rate yourself in each category.

How successfully did you:		
Visualize Window	**Hit the 3-Point**	**FB%**
1 2 3 4	1 2 3 4	1 2 3 4

Flashouts

Opponent/Ball/Bounce/Placement/Technique/Outcome

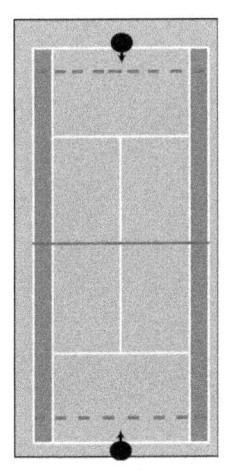

Drill 7

Circle where you would rate yourself in each category.

How successfully did you:		
Visualize Window	**Hit the 3-Point**	**FB%**
1 2 3 4	1 2 3 4	1 2 3 4

Flashouts

Opponent/Ball/Bounce/Placement/Technique/Outcome

PHASE III
Core Concept: Competing in the Zone

Competition takes on new meaning when you start competing in the zone. No longer are you competing against your opponent or the ball or the score. Instead, you are competing for the pure joy of playing the game.

Phase III shows you how.

Chapter 7: Competition

"Satisfaction lies in the effort, not in the attainment, full effort is full victory."
— Mahatma Gandhi

Key Subjects
7.1: Coming Out of a Parallel Mode
7.2: Leaving the Past Where It Belongs
7.3: Trust – Fear - Ego
7.4: Competition vs. Rivalry
7.5: Outcome-Based Competition
7.6: Process vs. Outcome
7.7: Winning the Real Competition
7.8: Seek and Ye Shall Find
7.9: The Spiritual Dimension of Tennis
7.10: The Now Drill

7.1: Coming Out of a Parallel Mode

When I teach people how to play tennis in the zone, there comes a time when they have to take what they have learned into a match. They have to do it for real, and that's when their ability to detach from the ball truly gets tested. That's when they find out if they can let go of their normal way of focusing and stay focused on their contact zone during the match.

Here's what always happens. All players can make the switch to their Parallel Mode in practice, but when they go to play their first match, they always have trouble maintaining the zone because they have trouble staying focused on their contact zone. It's not that they can't, it's that they won't. They don't trust the process enough to stay focused on their contact zone during competition. Players find that Fixed-Depth of Focus Input and their Parallel Mode work great in practice, but there's nothing on the line in practice. In practice the outcome doesn't matter. But in a match, when the outcome determines the score, players have trouble staying focused on their contact zone because they naturally want to focus on the outcome of their shots, which causes them to lose their fixed-focus and go back to Variable-Depth of Focus Input.

The end result is that they warm up in their Parallel Mode, using FDF, but when the scoring starts, they revert back to VDF and start playing in their Serial Mode. They warm up in the zone then compete in the norm. It happens every time.

You can imagine a student's concern when he has just finished taking a series of lessons on playing tennis in the zone in which he consistently experienced his peak performance state. Then, when he goes out to play a real match, he finds himself returning to his normal performance state!

"What the heck is the deal here? I paid good money to learn how to play tennis in the zone! But I go out to play a match and it doesn't work! What kind of crap is this? I paid for something that's supposed to make me play better in a match, but I'm playing just like before! What's going on? Why doesn't this Parallel Mode stuff work in a match? I want my money back!"

It never fails. People get into the zone in practice but they don't translate it to a match. Why is that? What is it about keeping score that makes competing in the zone so difficult?

Have you ever had a really great warm-up where you can't miss?

Everything feels great, your strokes, your timing, your contact – all working just the way they should. Yet the minute you start keeping score, your game begins to fall apart. It's like there are two different players out there on the court. There is the warm-up player who strokes the ball freely, who moves around the court effortlessly, who seldom misses a shot. Then there is the match player who gets tight during competition, who misses easy shots, who spirals down emotionally until the inevitable implosion. You feel like hiding but there is no place to hide, so you fold up instead and lose the match. Or, worse yet, you give up completely and tank the match to end the pain.

Guess what? Everybody who has played the game of tennis has gone through variations of this same theme. If they tell you they haven't, they're lying. Warming up well and then playing badly happens to all of us. People play great when there is no pressure, no scoring, nothing on the line. But the minute there is value placed on the outcome of the performance, a player's performance often suffers.

Why is that?

There are as many psychological reasons for this phenomenon as there are people who play the game, but when viewed from the perspective of system dynamics, all that has happened is that you have come out of your Parallel Mode of operation and returned to your Serial Mode of operation. And the reason you have switched back to a Serial Mode of operation is because you have come out of FDF and returned to VDF. You've gone back to focusing on the ball again.

Question: why did you go back to focusing on the ball?

Answer: because you are focusing on the *results* of your contact. You are focusing on the outcome. Once you place value on the outcome of a task, you will naturally want to focus on that outcome. You end up focusing on the outcome rather than staying focused on the process.

The best way to stay focused on the process of creating positive contact is to stay visually and mentally focused on the area of space and time in which contact occurs – your contact zone.

Flash-outs happen all the time when you first start using your Parallel Mode in a match. Instead of maintaining a fixed-focus on your contact zone, you start watching to see if your shots are going in or out, and once you start focusing on the outcome of your shots, you go right back to focusing on the ball. This visual switch from Fixed-Depth of Focus back to Variable-Depth of Focus results in an immediate switch back to a Serial Mode of operation, and with a Serial Mode of operation comes your normal performance state.

In the blink of an eye you have gone from playing tennis in the zone to playing tennis in the norm, and you lost the zone because of one simple reason: the need to see the outcome, the need to see if you were successful, your ego's need for instant gratification.

Looking to see if your shots are good is only human nature. We all want to know, right away, whether or not we were successful, and so we do what comes naturally. We watch the outcome. But as we watch the outcome, we also focus our eyes on the ball.

The instant we focus on the ball, for whatever reason, we immediately come out of FDF and switch back to VDF and our operating system switches immediately back to its Serial Operating Mode. We are no longer interfacing with the ball and the contact zone simultaneously, but we are back to interfacing with only the ball. We have lost our interface with the contact zone.

In that instant, we have also upset the balance of the temporal interface between past (ball) and future (contact zone) that was creating the reality of the present. The temporal dimension of the present is destroyed, and instead of maintaining the higher-order state of playing in the present, we go back to our normal state of playing in the past. The zone is gone – in the blink of an eye.

7.2: Leaving the Past Where It Belongs

Losing control of your focus is the rule rather than the exception. I have never seen a player who can immediately translate the maintenance of their Parallel Mode from practice to competition without first going through the frustrating process of switching back and forth between their Serial Mode and their Parallel Mode.

I understand their frustration because I had to go through it myself. I didn't just immediately switch over to playing tennis in the zone a hundred percent of the time, especially in matches. I'm just like everybody else; I was taught just like everybody else, and I was told, like everybody else, to watch the ball, to watch my shots to see if they went in, and to watch my shots in order to know where to position myself on the court. But I also watched my shots to make sure my opponent didn't cheat. Along the way, I was also told to watch my opponent carefully, to "read" him and anticipate his next shot. I was told to watch all the same things you were told to watch. But the one thing I was never told to watch was my contact zone. I was never told to focus on nothing.

There are plenty of valid reasons to watch all of the things we have been told to watch when we play tennis, but "watching" something and "seeing" it are two different visual processes. One process, seeing, involves opening your eyes to the visual stimuli in front of you. The other process, watching, involves focusing your eyes on something in your visual field. For instance, watching to see whether or not your shot goes in involves focusing your eyes on the ball as it hits the court.

What I found out through maintaining a fixed-focus on my contact zone was that I could still see everything that was happening in my visual field without watching or focusing on any of it. I also found myself getting into position much faster and anticipating much better when I didn't take the time to focus on my shots or on my opponent. As I became more adept at using my peripheral vision, I also got used to seeing what the game looked like when everything on the far side of my contact zone was blurry, including a blurry opponent hitting blurry shots and making blurry line calls.

Ironically, when I was focused on my contact zone, a bad call never upset me. Bad calls didn't bother me any more. I knew they were bad calls, but because I wasn't focused on them, I didn't give them any time, and when I didn't give them any time, they simply passed through my thought process without being given any value. By not focusing visually on my outcome, I gave it no focal value, thus no emotional value; the outcome was merely another aspect of a much bigger picture I was observing by staying in the present.

My shots, good or bad, my outcomes, good or bad, all carried the same value – none. They were all part of a unified whole, and it was this unified whole that took up my visual and mental focus. The more I practiced using FDF in my matches, the more I realized that I was getting better at competing in the zone. I could actually concentrate on maintaining the focus of my eyes during competition, and when I concentrated on my visual focus, I also found that there was no positive or negative value put on anything else occurring on the far side of my contact zone.

I found myself in this interesting place where what happened on the far side of my contact zone didn't affect me emotionally one way or the other. I was still aware of what was happening on the far side of my contact zone. In fact, I was more aware of what was happening than ever before. But instead of seeing only the part of the picture on which I was focused at that instant, I was seeing the whole picture at once, simply because I wasn't focused on any one part of it.

Of equal importance to the heightened state of visual and mental awareness I was sensing was the fact that my errors did not affect me negatively. When I missed a shot, I simply visualized the corrected contact event in my mind's eye and moved on to the next point. By consciously staying focally detached from the ball, I also stayed focally detached from the outcome of my shots. And by staying focally detached, I found that I was staying emotionally detached as well. A missed shot was simply that: a missed shot. I was too busy concentrating on the task of maintaining my visual and mental focus to give any time to the emotional baggage of missing a shot.

By remaining focused on my future depth of contact, I found that I was not focusing on my past mistakes. I was aware of them when they happened, but rather than mentally dwelling on them or trying to figure out what went wrong technically, as was my custom, I found that my mistakes could be left in the past where they belonged. All I had to do was remain focused on my future depth of contact. I was leaving the past in the past by focusing on the future.

The more I practiced maintaining visual and mental focus on my contact zone, the more sense it started to make. But, at first, because FDF input was so completely different for me, I found myself going back and forth between FDF and VDF during my matches. This switching back and forth between FDF and VDF was the most frustrating part of the learning process for me, and, as it turns out, it's the most frustrating part of the process for everyone who learns how to play tennis in the zone.

Eventually, I started trusting FDF and used it as my only input pattern during competition. I also started trusting that my operating system could perform in a Parallel Mode during a competitive match. In a Parallel Mode, I found myself able to perform at my highest level without thinking about everything I was told I had to think about if I was to play a thinking game of tennis.

To perform at your highest level is to perform without thinking about things first, to go on automatic pilot. I was finding that going on automatic pilot was no longer just a concept. It was happening to me more often and for longer periods of time, and it happened when I kept my focus fixed on my contact zone. I wasn't thinking about my position, I wasn't thinking about my strategy or my strokes; it was all just happening. I knew it was going to happen, I was aware of it happening when it happened, but I wasn't consciously thinking about it before it happened. Automatic pilot, also called action/awareness merging, is one of the components of flow.

7.3: Trust – Fear - Ego

The more accustomed I became to playing my matches in a Parallel Mode, the more I started to trust the process. Very simply, I played much better when I focused on my contact zone than when I focused on the ball. It's easy to start trusting a new process when it works better than the old process.

But that trust didn't come without a price. I was a fairly good player in my normal performance state. Granted, I was never invited to Wimbledon, but my trophy case wasn't a vacuum either. I was content with my rankings and I had always trusted the normal performance state that got me there, but deep down inside I had always felt that I was performing beneath my full-potential.

Do you ever feel that way? Like you aren't playing to your full-potential? You know there is something else within you, something better, something of deeper value, something you have experienced on those rare occasions when everything about your game comes together, when everything works. You know deep down inside, just as I knew, that this experience of the zone exists as a potential somewhere within you, but you just aren't sure how to access it.

Here's a question for you. If that potential exists within you; if it is there, if you are capable of achieving your full-potential, then what valid reason is there to settle for anything less?

This was one of the questions I asked myself as I practiced playing tennis in the zone, and there was only one answer I could find for being content with my normal performance state: fear.

I was afraid to step out of my comfort zone. I knew exactly what I could do in my normal performance state. I knew my limits, my parameters. I knew who could beat me and who couldn't. I knew my place. I felt safe. But in order to continue this process of learning how to compete in the zone, I had to give up that sense of safety. I had to let go of the security blanket I had clutched for so many years. My position in the tiny pond in which I swam was mine, and I damn sure didn't want to lose it. Not even if losing the security of that position meant finding a better position, a higher sense of security than I had ever known before. I was afraid to jump out of my little pond because I didn't know what to expect if I threw away my self-imposed limitations. I didn't know what lay outside the boundaries of my comfort zone.

I was afraid of the unknown, a natural enough fear. I knew what the past had brought me. I knew what to expect in my Serial Mode. But here I was, no longer focusing the way I had always focused – on the ball, on the past. Suddenly I found myself focusing on my contact zone, on the future, and, as we all know, the future, anybody's future, is unknown.

By focusing on my contact zone, I was forced to confront my natural fear of the unknown, my natural fear of the future, my fear of failure, and my negative expectations. All of the negative self-image issues that were a part of my life were suddenly being exposed, and I didn't like it one damn bit.

It was a dilemma for me. I could easily settle for the security of my normal performance state or I could take a chance, jump out of my little pond and reach for the unknown potential of my peak performance state. Should I continue to play tennis in the norm, or should I go all out and play tennis in the zone?

I chose the zone.

But the process of climbing out of my comfort zone didn't happen overnight, and it didn't happen without grieving what I left behind. My best friend and my worst enemy were one and the same – my own ego – and I had to leave my ego behind in order to find out who I really was in my peak performance state.

Dropping my ego wasn't easy, nor is it easy for anyone I teach. What I have found from years of teaching people how to play tennis in the zone is that this dilemma is the same for everyone who wishes to experience their peak performance state. We all have to pay the same price to see our full-potential, and the price we have to pay is the price of our own ego. It's a price that many players are unwilling to pay.

Is it any wonder kids have so much trouble reaching their full-potential? We put such high value on self-image that today's kids are unwilling to detach from their self-image no matter what the performance gain. A positive self-image is not a bad thing, mind you, but knowing when and how to drop your ego is key to peak performance.

I always tell my students that they will have to fight a very personal battle if they want to learn how to play tennis in the zone. That battle is the battle to detach from self, and we must all fight that battle if we want to experience our peak performance state.

Letting go of ego is such a simple concept on paper; yet to do so in practice is extremely difficult. Unselfconsciousness, loss of self, selflessness, whatever the name you give to dropping your ego at the side of the court, is a major component of the flow state, and it is perhaps the most difficult component to accept.

Getting comfortable with being selfless is like getting comfortable with a stranger. It's like asking yourself to become a child again. To play tennis in the zone is to see the game as a child sees the game; to play the game as a child plays the game. A child who doesn't know the rules, doesn't know how to score, doesn't know about technique and technology, doesn't care about logos, doesn't know about winning and losing. A child who knows only one thing: it's fun to hit a ball with a stick.

It doesn't matter how you do it. It doesn't matter what happens after you do it. It doesn't matter how expensive the stick is that you do it with, and it doesn't matter what you are wearing when you use your stick. All that matters is what you are doing at that moment in time, and what you are doing at that moment in time is making contact. One ball and one stick coming together at a common point in space and time to co-create contact.

Place your value on contact, on that event and that event only, and you will see what it is like to come into the tennis environment as a little child, selfless, uninhibited, and without fear.

Can any of us, as adults, say that we play the game with that kind of freedom?

I never could, until I started playing in the zone. That freedom, that selfless, fearless, uninhibited freedom we once experienced as children can be experienced once again in the game of tennis and in the game of life. It is one of the purest of human experiences, but it comes at the cost of your ego.

7.4: Competition vs. Rivalry

When we think of competition, we think of rivalry; me against you, one player trying to beat the other. That is the accepted notion of competition. But to compete in the zone is to play the game for completely different reasons, and beating your opponent is not one of them.

To compete in the zone is to detach from competition in the sense of rivalry and look at competition as a coming together with the game itself. That's what the word "competition" originally meant: to come together, to seek together, to agree.

No kidding…to agree!

Not much agreement in the competitive matches taking place on the tennis court nowadays. There's a lot of rivalry, very little coming together, and hardly any seeking together or agreement. That's the nature of today's competitive beast.

Competition is part of who we are and how we live. When you think about it, we compete every day of our lives: in our jobs, in school, in relationships, in sports. Most of the things we do contain an element of competition, and whenever competition is involved, performance is also involved. Tennis just happens to be one of many canvases on which we paint our competitive picture.

When you are in the zone, however, you are not competing in the normal sense of the word. You are not competing to win the tennis match. The outcome is not what the competition is all about. Whether you win or lose is not a part of your thought process. In fact, you might easily lose track of the score when you are in the zone. Scoring occurs, but because you are focused on something else, you give no weight to the score. Much like everything else in the zone, the score of the match is a part of your peripheral awareness and by detaching from the score, by focusing on something else, the score does not affect you, thus you are not affected by who is winning or losing.

As difficult as that is to believe, it's true. Being peripherally aware of the score is one thing; being acutely attached to the score is another. When you are in the zone, you don't have time to be attached to the score because you are continuously creating the dimension of the present, and when you are in the present you don't have time to be attached to or be affected by who is winning or who is losing. You are too busy staying in the present.

7.5: Outcome-Based Competition

Competition is difficult for everyone for basically the same reasons: we love to win, we hate to lose. Both winning and losing are outcomes and we put a tremendous amount of pressure on ourselves to produce a winning outcome. When I was a kid, I put so much pressure on myself to win that I had an ulcer at the age of fourteen. An ulcer! Talk about too much emphasis on the outcome! And I did it to myself. My problem was not with tennis; my problem was with myself. I wanted to be a winner so badly that I literally made myself sick. The need to be seen as a winner in my own eyes, in the eyes of my family, and in the eyes of my friends affected my performance every time I stepped on the court, and the sad truth is that most of the matches I won were won because I was so terribly afraid to lose.

My motivation as a kid was not the love of playing the game, or even the love of winning, but rather an intense fear of losing. I see the same motivation in many of today's juniors as well as many of today's supposedly mature adults. For whatever reasons, people equate losing a tennis match to being a loser.

Here's a fact: losing a match does not make you a loser, no matter some people might say. Likewise, winning a match does not make you a winner. That might be hard to swallow, but winning and losing are merely outcomes of an earlier process, and once you can separate the process from the outcome, you can start to put the emphasis where it belongs, on the process of performing, not the outcome of winning.

7.6: Process vs. Outcome

Somewhere along the line you have probably heard that in order to play your best tennis, you want to stay in the process and stay out of the outcome. Good advice from just about every coach and every sport psychologist in the game. But what, exactly, does it mean to stay in the process and out of the outcome? What is the process in tennis? What is the outcome? And how do you stay in one and out of the other?

First of all, the process in tennis is the action you take to create a contact event between the ball and your racquet. Making contact is the process. The outcome is what happens to the ball after you make contact. If you make positive contact, you get a positive outcome. The ball goes over the net and into the court. The point continues. If you make negative contact, you get a negative outcome. The ball goes into the net or out of the court. End result: the point ends. You lose.

The only other possibility is no contact, in which case your opponent made positive contact and you didn't get to the shot. You made no contact. The point ends and again, you lose.

Contact (+) = Outcome (+)
Contact (-) = Outcome (-)
Contact (0) = Outcome (-)

The only way to win in tennis is to make positive contact. That's the process, the cause. The outcome is the effect. Tennis is a very logical game of cause and effect, so how do you stay focused on the process, the cause, and keep from focusing on the outcome, the effect?

That's a tough one, especially when you are told from day-one to always keep your eyes focused on the ball. This traditionally accepted focal strategy creates a huge dilemma in tennis. If you are always focused on the ball, then you are locking yourself into a focal pattern that moves you back and forth between process and outcome. Focus on the ball as it comes toward you and you are focused on the process portion of the ball's movement. Focus on the ball after you hit it and, by definition, you are focused on the outcome portion of the ball's movement. So, if you are visually focused on the ball after you hit it, it is impossible to stay out of the outcome.

Fixed-Depth of Focus is a focal pattern in which you do not focus on the ball as it moves back and forth across the net, but rather you fix the focus of your eyes on your contact zone and let the ball move into and out of focus as it moves back and forth across the net. This FDF input pattern offers a logical solution to the process/outcome dilemma we all face whenever we play tennis. Not only is it a more efficient and accurate way to use your eyes, it is also a visual pattern that allows you to remain focused on the process and stay defocused from the outcome.

In short, by maintaining FDF as your input pattern, you automatically stay in the process and out of the outcome.

7.7: Winning the Real Competition

Competing in the zone is not about winning the match you are playing with your opponent, but rather about winning the match you are playing with yourself. If you don't believe that, just ask yourself one simple question: does your opponent usually win points by hitting outright winners, or do you lose points by hitting outright losers? Does your opponent usually beat you, or do you usually beat yourself?

If you really think about the matches you lose, you will realize that you beat yourself more often than your opponent beats you. The competition is really with yourself, and the easiest way to win the competition with yourself is to detach from self altogether, to become unselfconscious, selfless.

Self-doubt, fear, anxiety, stress, the need to be in control, all of the emotional angst you put yourself through, all of the mental wear and tear as well as all the damage you do to your spirit can be eliminated in one fell swoop.

How?

By letting go of self.

Where there is no self, there is no self-consciousness, no self-doubt, no worries, no anxiety or stress, no fear of failure or impatience to win. There is only the one-to-one relationship you form with the game when you play that game in the present. That's how you win the real competition out there on the court. You don't compete with your opponent. You compete with yourself, and you win that competition by letting go of self. When there is no self to compete with, you win the competition by default. Your toughest opponent is a no-show!

There's the real test. There's the real battle. And it's the battle you must fight if you intend to compete in your peak performance state. The competition on the court with your opponent is secondary. The primary battle, the primary competition is fought within you; the inner battle, the inner struggle, the Inner Game as Timothy Gallwey so eloquently put it.

Fighting this inner battle is a requirement of competing in the zone. Some people are willing to fight that fight, others are not. For those of you who are unwilling, there is a future filled with matches in which you continue to be your own worst enemy. Some days will be better than others, but for the most part, your matches will be played out in an arena where you not only have to battle your opponent, but you also have to battle yourself.

There is also the other side of the competitive coin, and for those of you who choose to fight and win the battle with yourself, you can look forward to a future filled with matches in which you are no longer beating yourself. Certainly there is still the secondary competition with your opponent, but the real battle has already been won. The primary competition has already been played-out in your favor.

Self only gets in the way of peak performance, it never helps out. The biggest favor you can do for yourself when you go out there to perform is to get yourself out of the way as fast as you possibly can and then maintain your selfless state for as long as you possibly can.

How do you get your self out of the way? By focusing on your contact zone.

When you are focused on your contact zone, you are focused on nothing, and when you are focused on nothing, self has nothing upon which to make comparisons. Self relative to nothing is "no self."

7.8: Seek and Ye Shall Find

What are you really looking for when you compete? If you are looking for trophies, power, money or even prestige, then certainly you must compete to find these rewards. But are any of them the ultimate prize? Or is there something else that you are looking for when you compete? Are you seeking yourself? Are you seeking something greater than yourself? Are you seeking anything other than a win?

These are questions that get to the root of competing in the zone and to the truth about the higher-order relationship that exists in the competitive environment, just waiting to be experienced.

However, in order to find this higher-order relationship you have to seek it in a different place. You have to stop searching in the same competitive arena. You have to look in a different arena altogether, and it's not an arena of familiarity. It's not the arena of your opponent and the ball and the court. It's not the arena of the material dimension. Instead, it's the arena of your contact zone and the Primary Contact Point: the arena of the non-material or spiritual dimension.

This kind of talk always makes people think you are a little bit crazy as a tennis professional, but when you look at the concept of a spiritual dimension to the game, what you are looking at is a dimension that is intangible, invisible to the naked eye. A dimension that is there, but you don't see it; a non-material dimension that exists in the tennis environment right along with the material dimension. Something that is there and not there at the same time: like your contact zone.

Your contact zone is the non-material dimension of the tennis environment, and the trick to finding a spiritual relationship with the game is to literally connect to that non-material dimension by visually and mentally focusing on it. In other words, you open the door to the spiritual dimension of the game by fixing your focus on "nothing."

By switching to FDF with its Parallel Interface you create an equal and simultaneous connection to both the material and non-material dimensions of the game, integrating them into the unified reality that is the game as a whole.

To compete in the zone is to create this higher-order relationship with the game as a whole, to be connected to both dimensions of the competitive environment - material and non-material - equally and simultaneously.

If all we seek as competitors is that which can be found in the material dimension of the game, then we will never come to the end of our search. The material search is all about having more of what the material dimension has to offer, and as we all know, the material dimension has plenty to offer, enough to keep us searching for a lifetime. For most people that's what the search is all about: more of the material dimension, more of the same thing. Thus the saying: "he who dies with the most toys, wins."

Here's another saying: "he who dies with the most toys was playing a lesser game."

Winning the most toys might be what the material dimension of the game is all about, but the spiritual dimension of the game has nothing to do with toys. Instead, it's about making a direct connection between you as an operating system and the spiritual dimension of the game.

"He who dies with the most spirit, wins."

7.9: The Spiritual Dimension of Tennis

I had always heard that the zone was the spiritual dimension of the game, and when I started studying the zone from the inside, I started to understand that there was indeed something special happening and it was something that not only transcended the performance boundaries of my game, but also the spiritual boundaries of my game. It wasn't like I suddenly became a better Lutheran because of the zone. The Missouri Synod had nothing to do with it. What was happening was that I was sensing a closer relationship with the game than I had ever known before, a transcendent relationship that, to me, held spiritual meaning.

Once I started going into the zone on purpose, I also started coming face-to-face with this spiritual dimension. I started to see, firsthand, what I had been hearing about and reading about for so many years. All of the talk about being one with the universe, being one with the game, being in the flow, all of the talk I used to think was nonsense was starting to strike a chord deep within me.

I knew there was something bigger and better out there in the tennis world, and that it involved something deeper and more meaningful in the game and in me, but in order to experience that deeper relationship with the game, I had to give up my normal relationship with the game. I had to stop relating solely to the material dimension of the game that was found in the ball and my opponent and the court, and start relating to the non-material or spiritual dimension of the game that was found through my contact zone and contact points. Everything about this higher-order relationship with the game was making sense to me on many different levels:

— There was the logic of the Parallel Mode with its Parallel Interface;
— There was the higher level of efficiency and accuracy displayed by my operating system when I was in a Parallel Mode;

- There was the equal and simultaneous interface with both the material and the non-material dimensions of the game;
- And most importantly, there was the creation of the temporal dimension of the present.

It was all starting to come together as I continued to go into the zone, and the more comfortable I became with getting into, maintaining, and competing in the zone, the more I understood that there was something required of me that had nothing to do with tennis and everything to do with me. In order to get into the zone at all, I had to let go of my ego. I had to get out of me, get out of self.

That was very difficult at first because my self-image, my ego, my whole sense of self relative to the game was tied up in my relationship to the material dimension of the game. Me relative to the ball; me relative to my opponent; me relative to the outcome; me relative to the score. There are many parts to the material dimension of the game, and I had been taught to focus on just about all of them.

I had never, however, been taught to focus on none of them, and by focusing on my contact zone, that's exactly what I was doing. I was taking my focus off the material dimension of the game and locking it firmly on the non-material dimension of the game.

Over time, instead of a relationship in which I experienced myself relative to everything material in the game, I found that I was experiencing myself relative to my non-material contact zone:

- Me relative to nothing.
- Self relative to nothing.
- No self.
- The selfless game that is the zone.

My total relationship with the game, visual, mental and physical, was now between me, my contact zone, and the Primary Contact Points – whenever and wherever they appeared.

But as I was forming this relationship with the non-material dimension of the game, I found that I was also forming a very positive relationship with the elements of the material dimension. In effect, I was forming a relationship with both the material and non-material dimensions of the game at the same time, which created an overall relationship with the whole of the game. The dualistic opposites of material and non-material were being integrated into the reality of a unified whole.

My sense of connection to the game was far greater than when I was in my normal performance state playing in my Serial Mode, and as I taught others what I was learning myself, they began to experience that same higher-order connection.

7.10: The Now Drill

What we have found is that "flashing out" on your own shot after contact is the primary cause of players coming out of the zone and returning to their normal performance state. In other words, focusing on your own outcome takes you away from focusing on your contact zone, not to mention taking you out of the process and putting you right square in the middle of the outcome. You can't stay in the process when you are focused visually and mentally on the outcome; yet flashing out on your own shot is the most common way you lose your focus when you first start playing tennis in the zone.

The fix for flashing out on your own shots is a drill we call the "NOW drill." It involves paying very close attention to what you are doing with your visual and mental focus immediately *after* you make contact.

The NOW drill goes like this: your objective is to keep your eyes and your mind focused on your contact zone immediately after you make contact, so your concentrative task is to say "now," out loud, when you are first aware of visually focusing on your window/contact zone after you make contact.

In a typical contact sequence you start by focusing on your window/contact zone, then you locate the contact point along the surface of your window and make contact at your contact point, and then you say "NOW" when you are first aware of visually focusing on your window/contact zone after contact.

This drill requires you to concentrate on your visual and mental focus before, during, and after contact. In other words, the NOW drill requires you to focus on what you are doing with your focus throughout the entire contact sequence.

As in the other zone drills, you start at mid-court and then work you way back to the backcourt. Again, the reason for this is to slowly increase your visual depth of field and get used to what it looks like to be focused on your contact zone instead of on the ball, your opponent, or any of the action across the net.

As in the other zone drills, moving from the midcourt to the back court will be difficult because you are so conditioned to focusing on your shots after contact, but by saying "now" at the moment you are aware of focusing visually and mentally on your contact zone, you will find that you get better at FDF as you become more aware of what you are doing with your focus before, during and after contact.

THE SEVENTH STEP

The Sixth Step was all about making contact with the 3-Point instead of making contact with the ball. Hitting the 3-Point creates a contact relationship with a non-material element of the game – the Primary Contact Point.

The Seventh Step is meant to expand on your relationship with the contact zone and thus deepen your connection to the non-material dimension of the game.

What draws players initially to the zone is not the fact that they will be opening the door to a spiritual relationship with the game. That's probably the last thing on their minds. What most players want out of the zone is a higher level of performance so they can win more matches. There is nothing spiritual about wanting to beat the ever-living daylights out of your opponent, and all things being equal, if you are in the zone and your opponent isn't, then there is no question as to who is going to beat the ever-living daylights out of whom.

Although winning is the initial draw, playing tennis in the zone, at its core, is not about winning. Instead, playing tennis in the zone is about you. It's about engaging your operating system in its most efficient and accurate operating mode, it's Parallel Mode, and then interfacing with the tennis environment in your Parallel Mode of operation. The shift to your Parallel Mode is why you play so much better when you are in the zone. But the spiritual dimension of the zone deals directly with the fact that you are "in the present," and when you are in the present, you are more likely to recognize the spiritual dimension of the game.

Every step in this book is about increasing your awareness of this non-material/spiritual dimension of the game, and if you have been following along, doing the steps in order, then you have been exposed to the spiritual dimension of tennis. You can't avoid it.

The Seventh Step is designed to further your awareness of your relationship with this spiritual dimension. It does so by making the non-material dimension of your contact zone, your imaginary window, as real as possible.

Question: How do you make an imaginary window as real as possible? Answer: By hitting it with a very real object – your racquet.

As you recall, the objective of the Sixth Step was to hit the 3-Point (a non-material element) instead of the ball (a material element), knowing that if you succeeded at hitting the 3-Point, you would also be creating a contact event between your racquet and the ball at the Primary Contact Point.

The Seventh Step furthers this objective by having your object of contact be another non-material element – your imaginary window. *So now, instead of contacting the 3-Point at your imaginary window, you contact your imaginary window at the 3-Point.*

In other words, hit your window, not the ball.

Practicing the Seventh Step

In the Seventh Step, your object of contact becomes your imaginary window and not the ball. Your objective is to make contact with the flat surface of your imaginary window (at the 3-Point) at the same time the ball makes contact with your imaginary window. (See Figure 8)

Figure 8

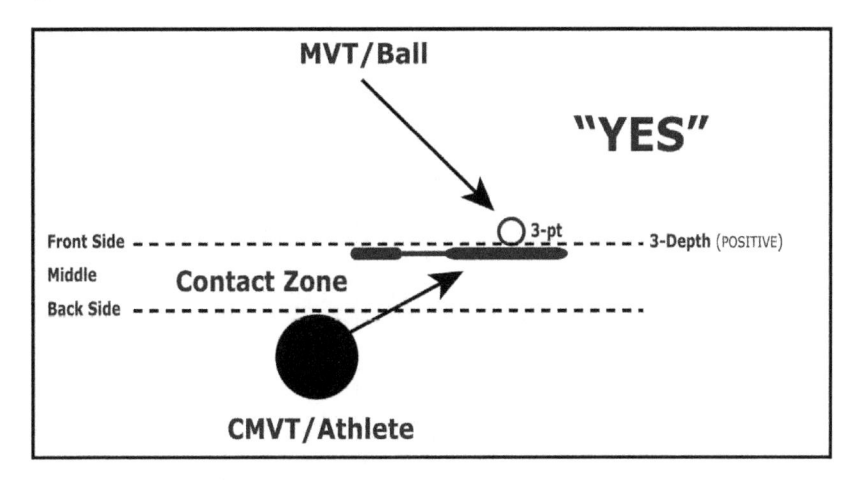

```
                    MVT/Ball
                        ↓
                                      "YES"

Front Side ------------------- ○ 3-pt ------ 3-Depth (POSITIVE)
Middle         Contact Zone   ↗
Back Side  ---------------- ●----------------
                            CMVT/Athlete
```

Your yes/no feedback is on making the distinction between hitting your window at the 3-Point versus hitting the ball. "Yes," if you hit the window, "no," if you hit the ball. In addition to solidifying your timing, this drill will help to solidify your technique by creating a flat racquet face at the contact event. The sensation is that you are hitting your window, not the ball.

Placement

To place your shots while in a Parallel Mode, it is necessary to stay focused on your contact zone. You cannot flash-out on the area of the court where you want to place your shot. If you look into the open court, even momentarily to see where you want to hit the ball, you have switched from FDF input to VDF input. That's a *flash-out on placement*, and when you flash-out on placement you come out of the zone.

In a Parallel Mode, placement can be achieved by simply "turning your window" perpendicular to the area of the court where you want your shot to go, and then swinging flat against your window at the 3-Point. The ball goes in the direction your window is pointed. (See Figure 9)

Figure 9

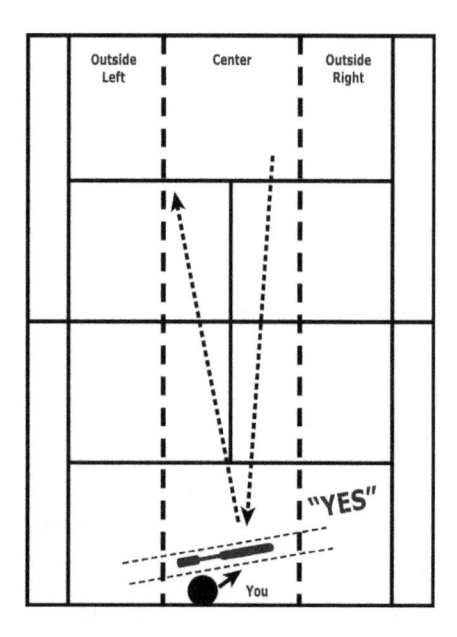

To begin learning placement in a Parallel Mode, it is suggested that you start by dividing the court lengthwise into thirds, giving you a center section, an outside-right section, and an outside-left section.

By turning your window toward the intersection of your imaginary line and your opponent's service line, you will give yourself a large margin of error and, with practice, you can pinpoint the angle of your window to land the ball closer to the lines.

As always, yes/no feedback helps to keep you focused on your contact zone as you learn to turn your window in the direction of your target. It also gives you immediate feedback on whether or not you have successfully achieved your objective.

A note of caution... When you first start learning to place your shots by turning your imaginary window, you will quite naturally start looking to see if your shots are going where you want them to go. While this is a natural visual response, the purpose of this drill is to practice making contact with your window at different angles, and by following the ball after contact, you are *flashing-out on the outcome,* which causes you to come out of the zone and return to playing tennis in the norm.

As you get more comfortable with FDF input, you will start seeing what the outcome looks like while you remain focused on your contact zone. You will also notice an emotional detachment from your shots as a result of your focal detachment from the outcome. To maintain a flow state, it is imperative to defocus from the results of your shots. Remember, you can still "see" the outcome without focusing on it.

FAQs on the Seventh Step

Q: What should I do if I flash-out on placement?
A: Assuming the ball stays in play, return your focus to your contact zone immediately and look for the 3-Point on the next shot. The sooner you return your focus to your contact zone, the sooner you return to FDF and a Parallel Mode.

Q: What flow components will I recognize when I hit my imaginary window instead of the ball?
A: While you will experience all of the flow components at one time or another, certain steps elicit certain flow components. In the Seventh Step you will notice:

- Clear goals,
- A sense of control,
- Total concentration on the task at hand.

Hitting your window is a clear goal. It feels like you are swinging the flat surface of your racquet against another flat surface; like you are using your strokes to hit your imaginary window instead of the ball.

Because you are not focusing on the techniques of the stroke, or the myriad of other things that happen during a contact sequence, the goal of hitting your window is clear and unambiguous amidst the clutter of everything else going on in the point.

As you get better at hitting your window, you are also learning to control your contact zone, and as you get better at controlling your contact zone, you will begin to feel a sense of control unlike any you've experienced before. Hitting your window instead of the ball is a deeply concentrative task, and by repeating this step, you will continue to develop your ability to totally concentrate on the task at hand, along with improving your on-court placement of the ball.

Q: How do I know if I'm successful if I am not looking at my own shot?

A: FDF input makes use of your peripheral visual system, so you will still "see" the results of your shot, even though your results will be out of focus. As you become more adept at hitting your window and letting go of the results, you will discover that it's not important to focus on the ball in order to play your best tennis.

Q: You mentioned detachment. Are you saying that I shouldn't care if the ball goes in the court or not?

A: I'm saying don't focus on whether the ball goes in or out. Keep your focus on your contact zone. The success or failure of your shot depends on what happens in your contact zone at the contact point. In this step, the primary goal is to focus on contacting your imaginary window at the 3-Point. This will produce a consistent, positive contact event, which in turn produces the desired results. Once contact has been made, the result of your shot is beyond your control, so rather than becoming focally and emotionally attached to something beyond your control, it is far better to attach your focus to something you can control - your contact zone.

Self-Rating Your Progress

The tasks you are measuring on the Seventh Step are:

1. Visualizing an imaginary window in front of you at a comfortable arm's length. (Visualize window)
2. Using your racquet to "hit" your imaginary window. (Hit the Window)
3. Immediate verbal "yes/no" feedback percentage. (FB%)
4. Identify your flash-outs

Your rating system for visualizing and hitting your window in each of the drills is the same 1-2-3-4 rating scale:

1. Never
2. Some of the time
3. Most of the time
4. Always

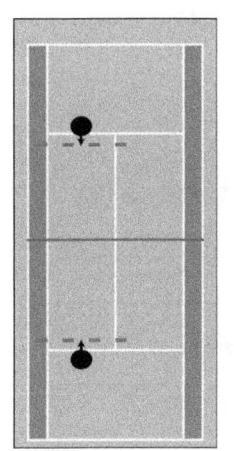

Drill 1

Circle where you would rate yourself in each category.

How successfully did you:		
Visualize Window	Hit the Window	FB%
1 2 3 4	1 2 3 4	1 2 3 4

Flashouts

Opponent/Ball/Bounce/Placement/Technique/Outcome

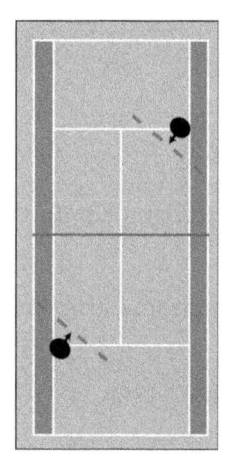

Drill 2

Circle where you would rate yourself in each category.

How successfully did you:		
Visualize Window	**Hit the Window**	**FB%**
1 2 3 4	1 2 3 4	1 2 3 4

Flashouts

Opponent/Ball/Bounce/Placement/Technique/Outcome

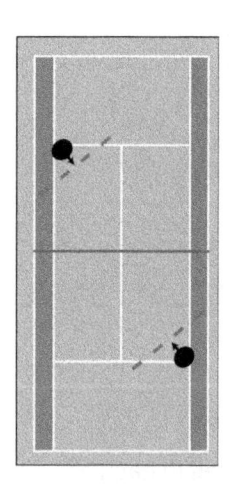

Drill 3

Circle where you would rate yourself in each category.

How successfully did you:		
Visualize Window	**Hit the Window**	**FB%**
1 2 3 4	1 2 3 4	1 2 3 4

Flashouts

Opponent/Ball/Bounce/Placement/Technique/Outcome

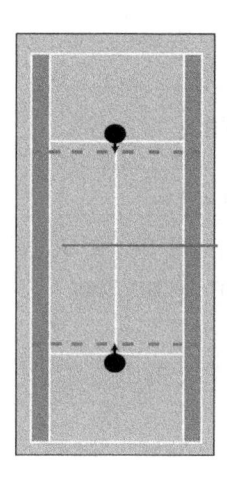

Drill 4

Circle where you would rate yourself in each category.

How successfully did you:		
Visualize Window	**Hit the Window**	**FB%**
1 2 3 4	1 2 3 4	1 2 3 4

Flashouts

Opponent/Ball/Bounce/Placement/Technique/Outcome

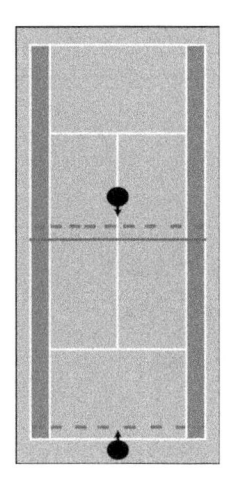

Chapter 7: Competition | 161

Drill 5

Circle where you would rate yourself in each category.

How successfully did you:		
Visualize Window	**Hit the Window**	**FB%**
1 2 3 4	1 2 3 4	1 2 3 4

Flashouts

Opponent/Ball/Bounce/Placement/Technique/Outcome

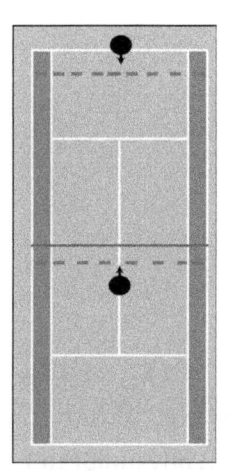

Drill 6

Circle where you would rate yourself in each category.

How successfully did you:		
Visualize Window	**Hit the Window**	**FB%**
1 2 3 4	1 2 3 4	1 2 3 4

Flashouts

Opponent/Ball/Bounce/Placement/Technique/Outcome

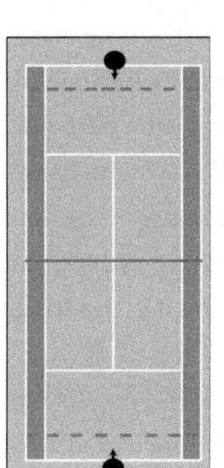

Drill 7

Circle where you would rate yourself in each category.

How successfully did you:		
Visualize Window	**Hit the Window**	**FB%**
1 2 3 4	1 2 3 4	1 2 3 4

Flashouts

Opponent/Ball/Bounce/Placement/Technique/Outcome

Chapter 8: Competing in the Zone

Live daringly, boldly, fearlessly. Taste the relish to be found in competition - in having put forth the best within you.
– Henry J. Kaiser

Key Subjects
8.1: The Battle
8.2: Controlling Your Emotions
8.3: The Parallel Mode Process
8.4: The Full Potential Experience

8.1: The Battle

Playing a tennis match should be fun. Competing should be fun. How's that for an outdated concept? Take a look at any junior tournament anywhere in the country and you'll see that the majority of kids competing out there are not having fun. Fun should not look so painful. Fun should not include screaming at yourself and calling yourself names. Fun should not include berating yourself, barfing before your matches, cheating your opponent to win, playing mind-games to psych-out your opponent. To watch a junior tennis tournament is to see everything that is wrong with competition. But, on those rare occasions, it is also to see everything that is right with competition.

The battle is what's right. The battle itself is good. The fight is fundamental. Movement versus Countermovement is natural. What's not natural is the way the fight gets fought. Parents interfere, coaches interfere, but mostly, players interfere with their own ability to fight the good fight. There are lots of things wrong with the game, but the game itself is not wrong. Nor is the natural competition inherent in the game wrong. In fact, competition is what makes the game right, and how you compete is what makes you a winner, not whether you win or lose.

Competition is about you and your opponent seeking something together within the game itself. The question is what are you and your opponent seeking together within the game? If you are seeking together to see who is the better player, then you are seeking out the lowest level prize the game has to offer. But if you are seeking together to find your highest-order performance state, your highest-order relationship to the game, then you have a chance to experience the highest level prize the game has to offer. You will find, however, that the highest level prize the game has to offer is not a prize at all. It's a one-to-one relationship with the game of tennis as a whole:

- A one-to-one physical relationship with the game,
- A one-to-one emotional relationship with the game,
- A one-to-one mental relationship with the game,
- And, at the pinnacle, a one-to-one spiritual relationship with the game.

This one-to-one relationship has been around since the beginning of time. It's a relationship known to every culture in the world, and we seek it out in many different ways. Sport is one of those ways, and tennis is a subculture of sport's larger population.

Being in the zone is contemporary slang for a human state of being that has played a major role in the development of man's religions, arts, architecture, and cultures. Human consciousness – higher-consciousness – is all about being in the present. Playing in the zone is being in the present on the tennis court and, as such, it is also about higher consciousness in tennis.

The mention of higher-consciousness makes some people uneasy. Others belittle the idea. But you simply will not experience your peak performance state if you are not in the temporal dimension of the present. You can play very well. You can even win all of your matches and take home all the trophies. But all that means is that you performed better than your opponents. It does not mean you performed to your full-potential.

For some of you, performing better than your opponents is all that matters. Trophies are all that matter. Trophies signify to others that you won the tournament; you were the best. But trophies do not signify whether or not you were *your* best. When you perform in your peak performance state, then, and only then, are you truly your best. That's when you are truly a winner, and the best part is that you don't have to win a trophy to win the biggest competition of all.

8.2: Controlling Your Emotions

Controlling your emotions during a match is a difficult task at best, but maintaining emotional control is one of the primary characteristics of competing in the zone, and the reason you maintain control of your emotions when you are in the zone is that you are continuously maintaining control of your focus.

Think about it. *What* is controlling your focus when you are focused on the ball? Whether you like it or not, the ball is controlling your focus, not you. When you focus on the ball, you are giving over control of your visual and mental focus to the ball. You are no longer in control of your own focus. Likewise, when you focus on your opponent, you are no longer in control of your own focus; your opponent is. Furthermore, while you are focused on your opponent, you are focused on your opponent's process, not your own.

On who's process would you rather be focused, yours or your opponent's? There's no surplus of available time out there when the ball is moving at high speeds, so if you want to stay in your own process, you might consider staying focally out of your opponent's.

Competing in the zone involves taking control of your own focus and literally fixing it on your contact zone. This takes practice, but as you get better at it, you will find that when you are focused on your contact zone, neither the ball nor your opponent controls your focus.

Instead, you do, and with your focus locked on your contact zone, you are simultaneously staying in the process while staying out of the outcome. To mix a metaphor, you are killing two birds with one focus.

The more you practice focusing on your own contact zone, the more you will find that you are gaining better control of your visual and mental focus as well as gaining better control of your emotions. Focal control and emotional control go together. You can't have one without the other. Nor can you lose one without losing the other. Lose control of your focus in a match and you will soon find yourself losing control of your emotions.

But taking control of your focus, like taking control of your backhand, requires practice; so when you get frustrated trying to control your focus, just remember how frustrated you were when you first tried to control your backhand.

There is, however, light at the end of this focusing tunnel. As you get better at controlling your focus, you will soon find that you are able to "see" everything that occurs on the other side of the net. You will be aware of your own outcome as well as your opponent's process without focusing on either of them. Remember, the most important event that occurs when you are competing on the tennis court occurs on your side of the net. More specifically, it occurs in your contact zone, at the point of contact. And by maintaining focal vigilance on your contact zone, your chances of being aware of the contact event are far greater than if you are focused somewhere else.

The contact zone is where it all comes together. The contact zone is where your process comes to its positive or negative conclusion and your outcome starts its positive or negative journey. The contact point is simultaneously an *Omega Point* where one contact sequence comes to an end and an *Alpha Point* where another contact sequence begins. Alpha and Omega, all rolled up into one contact point, and if you can be focused on that contact point when the event of contact occurs, you will soon come to know the freedom of competing in the zone.

8.3: The Parallel Mode Process

The world of sports performance has many approaches to the peak performance state. Like most approaches, the Parallel Mode Process is behavioral. But the Parallel Mode Process looks at the behavior of your operating system through a system dynamics approach to the zone, and that's what makes it different. You can get into the zone immediately by switching from your Serial Operating Mode to your Parallel Operating Mode.

But this systems approach to creating the zone is a two-edged sword. While switching to your Parallel Mode puts you in the zone immediately, it also creates a flow state in which you must continue to let go of self in order to maintain your Parallel Mode.

Being in the zone is a state that demands of you more than you might be willing to give. You must give up self completely in order to remain in the process and out of the outcome. You can't go halfway into the zone. You are either in the zone or you are not. There are no partials to the Parallel Mode Process.

For some people that's a turn-on. It's also what turns other people off. The turn-on comes when you are in the zone and performing at your highest level. The turn-off comes when you realize that you have to give up your normal conscious state in order to remain in the zone. Some people simply do not want to give up their normal conscious state because that state is where their ego resides. Their normal state is where they have come to know and cherish their self-image.

The first time players switch to their Parallel Mode is often the easiest for them because there is no pressure and no competition involved. Letting go of ego and self is easy when you are in a practice environment, an experimental mode where you have nothing to lose. But even the most intelligent and understanding people I know find it hard to let go of self and ego when the pressure to win is on.

Intelligence is not a requirement for playing tennis in the zone. A high I.Q. doesn't help you get into the zone. You just have to get in there and experience it. There's no other way to learn. Explaining the zone by defining its component parts is one approach to understanding the experience. But even a complete understanding of the parts of the experience will not create the experience itself. In order to create the experience of the zone, you must find a way to synthesize these component parts into a unified whole. That's where the Parallel Mode Process differs from other approaches. By switching to your Parallel Mode, your operating system interfaces with the tennis environment in such a way as to create the temporal dimension of the present, and the present is the temporal dimension in which the component parts of the zone are synthesized into the incredibly unified whole that is the experience of the zone.

Everyone who gets into the zone experiences a sense of power and connection to the game, although it affects some more deeply than others. For some, it's only about the fact that they play better when they are in the zone. For them, the challenge of the zone will be difficult at best.

The fact that they are taking up the process for the express purpose of the outcome means that they will go back to focusing on their results, which will immediately take them out of the zone. They will destroy the process before they truly get into it.

Too bad, because these players usually have a tremendous work ethic and strong personal values, but because their emphasis is on the outcome rather than the process, they will always keep focusing on the results of their contact. Sorry, but when you focus on the results, you go straight back to VDF and a Serial Mode of operation. No more tennis in the zone, just the ups and downs of tennis in the norm.

But for those of you who are seeking something deeper in the game and in yourself, making the switch to your Parallel Mode of operation will help you find exactly what you are looking for. Your Parallel Mode will allow you to access the spiritual dimension of the game; the same spiritual dimension that eludes you in your Serial Mode.

Those of you who learn to switch to your Parallel Mode will also learn to maintain the zone when you play. You will learn to detach from the outcome and become absorbed in the process.

Staying in the process and letting go of the outcome has an important operational underscore. To play tennis in the zone, to perform in your peak performance state, to experience a flow state, to stay in the process and out of the outcome, to do all of these things simultaneously, you must do one thing operationally. You must take control of your visual focus and fix it on your contact zone. Do that and nothing in the tennis environment will take control of your focus.

In an instant, you can go from letting everything in your environment control your focus to letting nothing in your environment control your focus. *And you can choose to let nothing control your focus by choosing to focus on nothing.*

Playing tennis in the zone is about performance, and your performance is directly related to your focus. Ask yourself this: *who or what is controlling your focus when you play the game?*

If you are focused on your opponent, the ball, or your outcome, then you are not in control of your focus. You might play well, depending on how well you can train your operating system to react to the fewest number of variables in your environment. But until you defocus from the people, places and things in your environment, you will not experience the full flavor of what the game has to offer. Until you take control of your own focus, you will not be able to experience the one-to-one relationship with the game that connects you equally and simultaneously to both the material and non-material dimensions of the game. Until you take control of your focus, you will not be able to play tennis in the zone.

8.4: The Full Potential Experience

When I teach people how to play tennis in the zone, I am teaching them to play the game to their full potential. So while the zone is about tennis, it's also about something more fundamental. It's about using their operating systems to their full potential. The end result is that they perform to their full potential as players and experience the game in a completely new and different way. Playing tennis in the zone is still playing tennis, but it is so different from playing tennis in the norm that the tennis part becomes secondary to the full-potential experience.

When you are in the zone you sense a stronger connection to the game, a much closer connection to the game than you have ever felt before. This closeness to the game creates a new and different sensation, and for some people that new and different sensation is more than they want to experience in their weekly adventures on the court. Their full-potential experience is too much of a responsibility for them and they choose to remain within the well-worn boundaries of playing tennis in the norm.

For others, however, the full-potential experience of the zone keeps calling them back. They want more. More newness, more sensation, more awareness, more of the closeness they feel to the game when they are in the zone. Even though it is difficult at first to detach from their comfort zone; even though it is difficult to focus on their contact zone instead of the ball; even though they are unfamiliar with their flow state, they keep coming back for more. And they keep coming back for the same reason I kept coming back at first: playing tennis in a Parallel Mode works better than playing tennis in a Serial Mode.

In time, players get into the zone for reasons other than the fact that they play better when they switch to their Parallel Mode. They get into the zone because they see something in themselves that can only be seen when they are in the present dimension. They see something in themselves that can only be experienced when they are interfacing with the unified whole that is the game of tennis.

That something that keeps drawing them back is the experience of a full connection to the tennis environment, a one-to-one interface with the game of tennis as a whole.

This one-to-one connection is available to everyone. It's right there for the taking, but it requires a major change in the way you connect to the game. Not everyone is anxious to make that change. Many players would rather work on improving their footwork dynamics than improving their system dynamics. Bear in mind that there is nothing wrong with improving the dynamics of your footwork. Good footwork is essential to playing tennis. Good footwork is not, however, essential to playing tennis in the zone.

What is essential is a Parallel Interface, and that means an equal and simultaneous connection to both the material and non-material dimensions of the game. It means an equal and simultaneous connection to both the past and future dimensions of the game. In other words, being one with the game is not about your feet, it's about the whole of your operating system connecting to the whole of the environment.

To play tennis in the zone, you must choose between playing in your Serial Mode or playing in your Parallel Mode. That choice involves a battle with your ego. In truth, some choose not to fight that battle. They are content with playing tennis in the norm.

Others choose to let go of their ego, to detach from self and connect with the deeper realities of the game. For them, there awaits more than just a better performance on the tennis court. For them, there awaits the full-potential experience of their operating system interfacing with the full-potential of the game. They are the ones who get to experience what the game of tennis is all about. They get to have the full-potential experience of playing tennis in the zone.

It can be had by anyone who plays the game - any game, at any level of competition. The key to experiencing your full-potential is to use the full-potential of your operating system to access the full-potential of your environment. That's the full-potential experience, the peak experience. We've all had peak experiences. The challenge is recreating them, then maintaining and stabilizing them.

The full-potential experience of playing tennis in the zone cannot be recreated in your Serial Mode of operation. Sorry. It just won't happen. A full-potential experience requires a full connection to the whole of your environment, and until you do something different in how you access the tennis environment, you won't experience everything the game has to offer. You might win the match. You might even win the whole tournament. You might hold a local, state, national or international ranking. You might even make a ton of money playing the game. But none of the material prizes you win come close to the whole story of what is available to you physically, emotionally, mentally and spiritually in a full-potential experience.

To be honest, most people will take a win over a full-potential experience any day of the week. Unfortunately, the environment does not offer you a win along with a full-potential experience. Wins certainly happen more often when you are performing to your full-potential, but the environment does not guarantee a win for being in the zone. The only guarantee you get is that if you give the environment your full-potential, then the environment will return the favor.

In the end, it's about choice. You can choose how you use your operating system to interface with the tennis environment. You can choose to focus on the ball and use VDF input to interface with the parts of the game sequentially in a Serial Mode of operation. Or you can focus on your contact zone and use FDF input to interface with the whole game simultaneously in a Parallel Mode of operation.

One way gives you a tennis experience. The other way gives you a full-potential tennis experience. In your Serial Mode, you get tennis in the norm. In your Parallel Mode, you get tennis in the zone.

It's your choice.

Either way, may you find happiness on your tennis journey.

For more information on the Parallel Mode Process please visit:
www.tennisinthezone.com

Bibliography

Gallwey, W. Timothy. *The Inner Game of Tennis*. Toronto: Bantam, 1979. Print

Jackson, Susan A., and Mihaly Csikszentmihalyi. *Flow in Sports. The Keys to Optimal Experiences and Performances*. Champaign, IL: Human Kinetics, 1999. Print

CPSIA information can be obtained
at www.ICGtesting.com
Printed in the USA
BVHW01s1532230218
508717BV00002B/169/P